Physical Charact[eristics of the] Shar P[ei]

(from The Kennel Clu[b])

Tail: Rounded, narrowing to fine point, base set very high. May be carried high and curved, carried in tight curl, or curved over. Lack of tail highly undesirable.

Body: Chest broad and deep, underline rising slightly under loin; back short, strong; topline dips slightly behind withers then rises over short, broad loin.

Hindquarters: Muscular, strong; moderately angulated; hocks well let down.

Coat: Distinctive feature of breed. Short and bristly; harsh to touch. Straight and off-standing on body, generally flatter on limbs. No undercoat.

Colour: Solid colours—black, red, light or dark shades of fawn and cream.

Feet: Moderate size, compact, toes well knuckled. Fore and hind dewclaws may be removed.

Size: Height: 46–51 cms (18–20 ins) at withers.

Shar Pei

by Juliette Cunliffe

Contents

History of the Shar Pei..........................9

A true survivor, the Shar Pei has prevailed despite the destruction of Chinese breeding records and the extermination of the canine population in China in the mid-20th century. Travel back in time to China's Han Dynasty and trace this ancient breed's progression from fighting dog to rare breed to prized pet and show dog that is recognised and revered around the world.

Characteristics of the Shar Pei..................20

His regal scowl and his distinctive wrinkles are but two of the traits that make the Shar Pei unique in dogdom; learn also about his personality, which combines confidence and independence with affection and devotion to people. Also discuss caring for the Shar Pei and health considerations in the breed of which every prospective owner should be aware.

The Breed Standard for the Shar Pei............30

Learn the requirements of a well-bred Shar Pei by studying the description of the breed set forth in The Kennel Club standard. Both show dogs and pets must possess key characteristics as outlined in the breed standard.

Your Shar Pei Puppy..........................38

Be advised about choosing a reputable breeder and selecting a healthy, typical puppy. Understand the responsibilities of ownership, including home preparation, acclimatisation, the vet and prevention of common puppy problems.

Everyday Care of Your Shar Pei.................68

Enter into a sensible discussion of dietary and feeding considerations, exercise, grooming, travelling and identification of your dog. This chapter discusses Shar Pei care for all stages of development.

Shar Pei

Housebreaking and Training Your Shar Pei........88

by Charlotte Schwartz
Be informed about the importance of training your Shar Pei from the basics of housebreaking and understanding the development of a young dog to executing obedience commands (sit, stay, down, etc.).

Health Care of Your Shar Pei....................117

Discover how to select a proper veterinary surgeon and care for your dog at all stages of life. Topics include vaccination scheduling, skin problems, dealing with external and internal parasites and the medical and behavioural conditions common to the breed. A special section on common eye problems is provided for the new owner's reference.

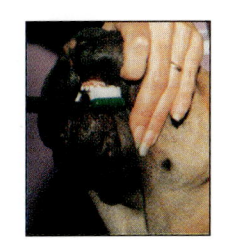

Index........156

PUBLISHED IN THE UNITED KINGDOM BY:

INTERPET
PUBLISHING

Vincent Lane, Dorking
Surrey RH4 3YX   England

ISBN 1-902389-44-1

All rights reserved.
No part of this book may be reproduced in any form, by photostat, scanner, microfilm, xerography or any other means, or incorporated into any information retrieval system, electronic or mechanical, without the written permission of the copyright owner.

Copyright © 2000 Animalia, Ltd.   Cover patent pending. Printed in Korea.

PHOTO CREDITS:

Norvia Behling, TJ Calhoun, Carolina Biological Society, Doskocil, James Hayden-Yoav, James R Hayden, RBP, Bill Jonas, Carol Ann Johnson, Alice van Kempen, Dwight R Kuhn, Dr Dennis Kunkel, Mikki Pet Products, Antonio Philippe, Phototake, Jean Claude Revy, Alice Roche, Dr Andrew Spielman.

The publisher wishes to thank Cindy Cullinane, Marylen Daly, Jeffrey Grieco, Leslie Michaels, Joan T Miller, Eleanor B Paulus, Wendy Schaber, Maryann Smithers, Natacha Vezinaud and the rest of the owners of dogs featured in this book.

8 • *Shar Pei*

The Chinese Shar Pei has captured the passions and imaginations of fanciers around the world. From their darling wrinkled appearances as puppies to their profound, unusual expressions as adults, Shar Pei continue to win new admirers every year.

History of the SHAR PEI

Although now an increasingly popular Chinese breed, there is varying opinion as to the actual origin and uses of the Shar Pei, for little has been well documented through the centuries. To add to the dilemma, around 255 BC documentation about China's canine population was destroyed by the Emperor Ch'in Shih.

What we do know is that there have been many periods throughout history when the Chinese have been interested in breeding dogs. Their dogs were sometimes kept merely as companion animals, but others were used in hunting, and frequently as a source of meat, leather and pelts.

The history of the Shar Pei goes back to China's Han Dynasty (206 BC–220 AD), with statuettes of tomb dogs resembling the breed. These clay figurines are of square-bodied dogs with short legs, a curled tail and a scowling expression. Vases of the period also depict sturdily built dogs with short, erect tails and short legs that may have some connection with the Shar Pei we know today.

Sharing a bluish-black tongue and Oriental beginnings, the Smooth Chow Chow probably played a major role in the development of the Shar Pei.

The Rough Chow Chow is the more popular variety of this Chinese breed. It is said that the breed's name derived from the Chinese slang for something edible ('chow'), as in ancient times these dogs were sometimes kept for food.

ANCESTRY

It is generally believed that the Chow Chow has played an important part in the Shar Pei's history, not least because both breeds share the unusual blue-black tongue. The Tibetan Mastiff is also an ancestor of the Shar Pei, and it is quite possible that some of the other mastiff breeds also lie somewhere in the background. When looking back to the breed's past, we should bear in mind that during the Han Dynasty the Roman Empire was rapidly expanding and trade routes were opened up across Central Asia. Such routes would have allowed dogs from Rome's colonies to find their way to China, along with other items of trade.

It is commonly believed that another breed that might well have played a part in the make-up of the Shar Pei is the Pyrenean Mountain Dog, because some Shar Pei have double dew claws like the Pyrenean. However, double dew claws can be found on many different breeds, including those in France, Mongolia and other Asian regions.

EARLY FIGHTING DOGS

The fountainhead of the breed appears to have been Dah Let (also written as Tai Leh), situated in the Kwan Tung Province, near Canton in southern China. A close

History

The Pyrenean Mountain Dog is counted among the Shar Pei's ancestors because it is one of the few dogs that share the double dewclaws.

ancestor of the breed is undoubtedly the Dah-Let Fighting Dog, which, as its name implies, was used for fighting purposes. Its jaws were powerful and hence easily able to grasp an opponent, while its stiff coat was uncomfortable for an opponent to hold in its mouth, another advantage when fighting. In fact the Shar Pei can use its coat for defence, stiffening the hairs even more when required.

In the early fighting dogs, flexibility of skin was also highly useful, for this provided the facility to turn and manoeuvre so that another dog's hold could be broken easily. Because the skin was thick and spongy, damage to underlying tissue was prevented. Wrinkle was also important for protection, though if in excess it could too easily be torn. Some of the

> **AN EDUCATION**
> Hong Kong's Nelson Lam makes a great effort to educate people about the Shar Pei. His personal preference is for a Shar Pei of 56 cm (22 ins) and weighing 25 kg (55 lbs). He has, though, listened objectively to other opinions and has reached the decision that the Shar Pei can reach 58.5 cm (23 ins).

The rare Tibetan Mastiff has been closely associated with the development of the Shar Pei.

very early Shar Pei's ears were said to have been as small as a thumbnail, only large enough to cover the opening of the ear. Such a tiny ear was also useful in a fight, for the attacker had nothing to grasp.

Dog fighting was a pastime of farmers and small town dwellers, for they had little else by way of entertainment. The breed has been described as having all the features of a gladiator, but in character the Shar Pei is not a born fighter. However, if owners provoked their dogs to fight from a very early age, they reputedly enjoyed the sport.

There are various fine examples of fighting dogs made in Chinese porcelain during the Ch'ien Lung Dynasty (1736–1795). Many of these

RESEMBLING THE CHOW
One of the earliest Shar Pei breeders, Mr Jones, a Chinese breeder who later retired to Canada, told Nelson Lam that he used the Smooth Chow Chow to mate to the Shar Pei. This is surely one of the reasons why some Shar Pei today resemble that breed.

History   13

Fanciers admire the Shar Pei's unusual characteristics that make it unique in the dog world. The Chinese also developed goldfish with distinctive physical traits including missing fins, bulging eyes, growths on the head, etc. The inset shows a Chinese Water Bubble-eye Goldfish, which is missing a dorsal fin.

closely resemble the Shar Pei we know today, although they do not display so much wrinkle and those I have seen have bushy tails.

Dogs of the size and character of the Shar Pei were, however, no match for the larger, heavier breeds that had made their way to China. Indeed, it was often said that the Shar Pei had to be given artificial stimulants to improve its instinct to fight. Today the breed has a much more gentle nature, and mentally most are far removed from their ancestors.

One should also remember that in China any dog which protected property used to be called a 'fighting dog,' so it is very possible that the term remained in use long after the Shar Pei's fighting days were over. Although certainly used as a fighting dog by pirates and sailors in ports, the breed soon became a multi-purpose dog, used also as a guardian of the home and for hunting, particularly the wild pig. It is most unlikely that the Shar Pei was ever used to retrieve as it has an instinctive habit of shaking anything it catches.

MORE DESTRUCTION OF RECORDS

China's complicated history moved on. The Han Dynasty,

> **THE PEOPLE'S NEEDS**
> Mr Tsang Pong Shing was a dog trainer, pig farm worker and, later, a pet shop trader who sold dogs according to people's needs when trading in the 1940s. He dealt with many Shar Pei and, interestingly, used the Shar Pei for vermin hunting.

during which dog ownership had been at its height, ended. There was still more destruction of records, material that would have been so valuable for researchers in years to come. Typical of the destruction were the actions of the one-eyed Emperor Yuan who lived during the 13th and 14th centuries. In the knowledge that he was to be killed, he set fire to all of his 140,000 ancient books, rather than allow them to fall into the hands of those he considered unworthy. It is also of great interest to note that he would

> **FIXING A MISTAKE**
> According to Nelson Lam, the Bulldog is evident in the modern type of Shar Pei and some irresponsible breeders used the Pug in an endeavour to rectify their mistake. This explains why some dogs in the West have a shorter neck and are smaller than the original type.

not allow pottery figures of dogs to be placed in his grave, even though that was the custom of the day. By the end of the Ming Dynasty in 1644, the interest in dogs had lessened considerably and numbers of dogs of most breeds had fallen into severe decline.

EXCHANGE BETWEEN EAST AND WEST

Although there was a period of two hundred years, beginning from the mid-14th century, in which commerce was curtailed, there have always been trade relations between East and West. A Russian ambassador in China in the late 17th and early 18th century took with him his dogs, some of which were hounds. Added to situations such as this, it is well known that dogs were often used as tribute gifts between emperors and kings.

THE COMMUNIST REGIME IN CHINA

From 1949 when China was taken over by Communist rule, heavy fines were imposed for keeping dogs of all kinds, for dogs were considered luxury items. Later Mao Tse-tung decreed that pets were symbols of the privileged classes and because of this he ordered their mass extermination. Consequently, the canine population was decimated in the cities, but in outlying countryside areas thankfully some dogs still survived.

Just a few small pockets of Shar Pei were still alive in 1950, these having been smuggled to rural areas of Hong Kong, Macao and Taiwan.

THE 1970s ONWARD

Before the 1970s it is certain that there were only very few Shar Pei surviving, but in the early 1970s a small group of people decided to set about preserving the breed. This positive-thinking group of people, which included Mr C M

The Shar Pei has gained a following in the West as a show dog and companion, roles that the breed historically did not play in its homeland. This Shar Pei took home ribbons at the famed Crufts Dog Show in 1999.

Shar Pei come in a variety of colours. This lovely black bitch is Konishiki Ace of Spades.

Chung, a breeder of Shar Pei, and the young Matgo Law, searched desperately for representatives of this fast declining breed. They did not manage to acquire large numbers, but what they did find basically formed the foundation of the breed we now know. By then the breed was considered 'endangered,' so Shar Pei were re-located to Hong Kong to establish a breeding programme.

As there were so few Shar Pei from which to choose, all available bloodlines were used and this involved frequent use of dogs without known pedigrees. Inbreeding was used in an aim to produce dogs that resembled the original type of Shar Pei as closely as possible. At this early stage in the breed's re-formation, breeders concentrated firstly on producing dogs that were typical; soundness was secondary.

When typical Shar Pei had been produced, a breed standard was drawn up and this gave an eminently clear picture of the breed produced by those from the breed's homeland.

THE SHAR PEI IN AMERICA

A puppy bred by Mr C M Chung was exported to the USA in 1966 and this was the first known Shar Pei to have arrived in America. His name was 'Lucky.' Five Shar Pei went to the USA between 1966 and 1967, but there was initially little interest in the breed. Officially known at that time as the 'Chinese Fighting Dog,' the breed had its first real exposure to the Western world in 1971.

In an article about rare breeds, a canine magazine included a picture of a Shar Pei, stating that it was probably the last surviving specimen of the breed. The article prompted no reaction, but in 1973 Matgo Law wrote an article entitled 'Chinese Fighting Dogs' in America's *Dogs* magazine. He expressed his concern about the fate of the breed, especially as Hong Kong would revert to Communist Chinese rule at the end of the century.

Numerous enquiries were received as a result of the article and potential buyers' requests were too numerous to be filled. However, this was to mark the real beginning of imports to America from Hong Kong, Macao and Taiwan.

Early imports varied widely in type. Not only did some carry genetic problems but many had major faults. It was clear that this new and unusual breed was seen by some as an opportunity to make money, and several early breeders seemed content to produce merely the largest number of dogs in the shortest possible time.

Thankfully, there were some dedicated Shar Pei enthusiasts among those early owners, some of whom were already knowledgeable breeders of other breeds of dog. Much experimentation in breeding was carried out in the early years and there was enormous disparity in type, some clearly not conforming to the breed standard that had been laid down.

By 1974 enough Shar Pei had been imported to the USA for the decision to be made that a breed club be formed. This would provide an opportunity to pool both knowledge and experience in the breed's formative years. The first meeting of the club was held in Oregon on 26 April, 1974, with a second meeting in July of that same year. The possibility of registration for the breed with the American Kennel Club (AKC) was discussed. By 1976 thirty breeders of Shar Pei were known in the USA, although not all were club members. Then the official name of Chinese Shar Pei was decided upon, and the breed standard was revised. Interestingly, minimum prices were also set for the sale of puppies and for stud fees.

Until then there had been few opportunities to show the breed, but by 1978 there were sufficient numbers being exhibited to put on a speciality show. In the 1980s numbers grew dramatically, and several hundred could be exhibited at a national speciality show.

The breed standard was further revised in America, with references to fighting dogs and to the Chow Chow being deleted. This new standard came into force in 1982 but there have been various revisions since then.

A major landmark came in the Shar Pei's history on 8 May, 1988, when the breed was accepted by the AKC into its Miscellaneous class and the first American Shar Pei gained its championship title in 1992.

Not just the continental USA has been enjoying and promoting the Shar Pei. The breed had reached Hawaii in 1970 and has been in the Philippines since the 1980s.

THE SHAR PEI IN BRITAIN

The first Shar Pei import to Britain, Heathstyle Dandelion, arrived in 1981. This fawn dog was bred in the USA and imported into Britain by Heather Ligget. Not only did he appear on several television shows but, more importantly, sired top winning specimens of the breed. Later that same year Heather Ligget imported a bitch, Down-Homes Junoesque of Heathstyle, this time from Hong Kong's Matgo Law. These two imports, mated together, produced the very first litter of Shar Pei puppies in Britain.

Several other Shar Pei bloodlines were imported and, as in the USA, in the early years there were considerable variations in type as there was a lack of background information regarding ancestry. Fourteen representatives of the breed were registered with The Kennel Club in 1982, and by this time there was already a waiting list for puppies. It was therefore felt that the time had come to form a breed club, but it took a further four years before the Chinese Shar-Pei Club of Great Britain was officially recognised by The Kennel Club. The Club's magazine, *The Wrinkle*, was first published in 1984 and has provided a valuable link for members. As well as other events, this club also holds educational seminars, of particular value to judges of the breed.

Another enthusiastic club for the breed is the Midland Shar Pei Club (Proposed). This was set up in 1992 and its large membership enjoys an active programme of events, but the club is still seeking the official approval of The Kennel Club.

The first Open Show for Shar Pei was held in conjunction with the Rare Breeds Spectacular in 1987, and in 1990 the Shar Pei had breed classes scheduled at Crufts Dog Show. The Kennel Club permitted Challenge Certificates to be allocated to the breed in 1999, allowing Shar Pei to compete for the title of Champion.

THE SHAR PEI AROUND THE WORLD

Although not found in any great numbers in other countries of the world, the Shar Pei is now represented in many nations, including Australia, Canada,

> **FACT OR FICTION?**
> According to some reports, Shar Pei have supposedly encountered wild boar in the New Territories of Hong Kong and in China, and have also been used to chase big cats. However, other experts on the breed think such incidents are unlikely.

History

New Zealand and South America. It is particularly strong in Germany, where the first Shar Pei was imported into Europe by Joachim Weinberg.

The breed is still actively bred in Hong Kong and breeding from Hong Kong has had a substantial influence on the Shar Pei in Japan.

This top-winning bitch in the UK is exemplary of the rapid development of quality Shar Pei around the world.

Characteristics of the
SHAR PEI

It is easy to see why the Shar Pei now has so many devoted followers. Not only is this an unusual-looking breed that, once seen, is rarely forgotten, but it also has many endearing characteristics.

However, it must be stressed that the Shar Pei is not a breed that suits everyone. The breed has had much publicity, largely due to its unique appearance, but publicity is not always a good thing and prospective owners should seriously do their 'homework' before deciding that a Shar Pei should share their lives.

PHYSICAL CHARACTERISTICS

The Shar Pei is best known for its loose skin and frowning expression, with its rather large head and unique, well-padded muzzle, bulging slightly at the base of the nose. There is also padding on the lower lip, but this should not be so excessive as to interfere with the bite.

This is a substantial, strong, squarely built dog, with dogs being more powerful than bitches. According to the British breed standard, height should be between 46 and 51 cms (18–20 ins) at withers, though certainly both taller and shorter Shar Pei are to be found, particularly when one looks at the Shar Pei population in the world as a whole.

Another important breed characteristic is the Shar Pei's bluish-black tongue. On closer investigation you will find that the flews, roof of mouth and gums are also black, though lighter colours are permissible in cream and light fawn dogs.

COLOURS AND COAT

A litter of Shar Pei can comprise puppies of several different colours. Those accepted within the British breed standard are the solid colours, black, red and light or dark shades of fawn and cream. Frequently there is lighter shading on the tail and back of thighs, but a dog patched with white or spotted is undesirable. As solid colours are desired, the black and tan colour combination that crops up from time to time is not a recognised colour.

The coat is another highly distinctive feature of the breed and sets the Shar Pei apart from all other breeds of dog. It is said that the name 'Shar Pei' means 'sandy-coated dog,' a description relating to the texture of the coat, not to its colour. It is short, bristly and harsh to the touch.

Indeed, some of the very short coats in the breed, known as 'horse coats,' can sometimes irritate human skin, so one should be fully aware of this before deciding on a Shar Pei puppy. Of course, not everyone is allergic to the coat, but this should be considered and reactions assessed before making a long-term commitment to the breed.

The coat has no undercoat, is straight and stands off from the body, but is generally flatter on the limbs. Coats over 2.5 cms (1 in) long are undesirable.

Although no different types of coat are mentioned in the breed standard, in reality they differ considerably. An authority in Hong Kong even suggested that there are as many as ten different coat types in Shar Pei and the subject has certainly been a controversial one in recent years.

Looking back to the Hong Kong Kennel Club standard, a clear description of why the Shar Pei's coat was to be harsh was explained as it is was to be 'absolutely too uncomfortable to be held in any canine mouth.' Some coats, known as 'brush coats,' are longer but still conform to the standard; others are called 'bear coats.' The latter

GROWING INTO THEIR SKIN

Shar Pei puppies should have much fuller, more wrinkled skin than they will have in adulthood. One has to admit that they look absolutely adorable as puppies, seeming to grow into their skin as they mature.

are much longer and softer and are uncharacteristic of the breed, resulting from throw-backs to other breeds which were used in re-developing the breed as we know it today.

TAILS AND DEWCLAWS

The tail of the Shar Pei is set extremely high and is never docked; even the breed standard states that a lack of tail is highly undesirable. The tail itself is rounded and narrows to a fine point, but may be carried in different ways. It can be high and curved, carried in a tight curl, or curved over.

Dewclaws on front and hind feet may or may not be removed, this being left to the discretion of the breeder. However, if they are removed, this should be done when the puppies are three days old.

PERSONALITY
Active and alert, the breed has a calm, independent nature and is very affectionate. The Shar Pei is devoted to people and loves to live as an integral part of the family, but one should always bear in mind that the breed might not necessarily be so friendly toward strangers.

The Shar Pei is very much an Asian breed, and like others from this region is usually prepared to protect both its home and owners. Alert to the slightest sound, it is quick to come between its much-loved owners and anyone it considers may be a threat. However, in most cases, the Shar Pei is content to pin down any adversary, rather than to bite.

This is not generally an aggressive dog, but it is always important to consider that a Shar Pei is capable of doing damage, so must be trained from an early age to know what is and is not acceptable behaviour.

The Shar Pei is a good guard dog, for this behaviour is instinctive in the breed. And although the breed's fighting days are long since past, one should always keep in mind that ancestors of the present-day Shar Pei were used for fighting, so any tendency displayed in this regard should be kept well under control.

Another aspect of the breed's nature, about which one should be aware, is the hunting instinct. They have very good eyesight and employ great patience in stalking their prey.

> **TALES OF THE TAIL**
> Tails of Shar Pei vary quite considerably. Frequently a puppy's tail does not curl until it is older, but even a puppy's tail should be set high, as is correct for the breed, and it should be thick at the base.

Characteristics

A Shar Pei is an inventive dog, and will undoubtedly provide its owners with many hours of fun and amusement, especially while growing up. This breed enjoys playing games, both with other dogs and with humans, and it can be absolutely fascinating to watch a Shar Pei think things out before apparently deciding on the most appropriate action to take.

HEALTH CONSIDERATIONS
The Shar Pei is not a breed without health problems; fortunately, dedicated breeders have done their best to eradicate problems that have occurred in the breed and their efforts have paid dividends.

SWOLLEN HOCK SYNDROME
Swollen hock syndrome is of particular concern with the Shar Pei. It can also be known as familial Shar Pei fever and systemic amyloidosis. Although a dog may show no signs of the disorder, it can be carrying it genetically, so two dogs mated together, both with the defective genes, can produce puppies that either have, or carry, the syndrome.

The disorder is caused by inability to break down and remove amyloid protein. Instead this protein builds up, eventually taking all life out of the kidneys and liver. In consequence, Shar Pei that are so affected die at an early age from either liver or kidney failure.

Symptoms are lethargy, poor appetite and sometimes a high temperature, combined with shivering. The breed's large muzzle may also be swollen and the eyes puffed up, symptoms

WRINKLE CARE
Because of the Shar Pei's wrinkles, it is important to take special care of the skin. Ensure that particles of food and dirt do not get trapped in the wrinkles, for this can easily set up an irritation.

> **COMMON MANGE**
> Demodectic mange is the most common type of mange found in the Shar Pei. Caused by parasitic mites thriving in hair follicles, some dogs have an inherited inability to resist them. An early sign is the appearance of small bald patches, with the skin later becoming reddened and scaly.

similar to a wasp sting. The dog may scream in pain when the muzzle is touched. The joints can be stiff and the dog may have difficulty in placing either or both of its hind legs on the ground. The back legs can become swollen and thickened.

Yet another sign in puppies that are affected is a roached back, due to abdominal pain. The puppy may also vomit and have diarrhoea.

Attacks occur with varied frequency. They might have an attack virtually every week, or else they may have only a couple and then never again. However, even if the attacks are few, the cause must be thoroughly investigated and if the reason is swollen hock syndrome, the dog in question must be eliminated from breeding programmes.

The usual age at which the syndrome affects Shar Pei is between 4 and 18 months, but it has been known earlier and others have shown no sign until adulthood.

To alleviate the discomfort as much as possible, the temperature must be kept normal. One can wash behind the ears and the dog should be kept in a cool, quiet room. The dog should not be forced to eat food, but drinks of honey water are good.

Keeping an affected dog on a low-protein diet (16–20%) is beneficial, and natural sulphur can help to purify the system. Fresh parsley can help the kidneys.

ENTROPION

Entropion is a rolling in of either one or both of the eyelids, and good breeders are trying hard to eliminate this problem from the breed. It causes constant irritation to the eye as the eyelashes come into contact with the cornea.

Although by no means a problem specific to the Shar Pei, the cause in this breed is usually an excess of wrinkle around the eye. Sometimes the problem can be so severe that a baby puppy's eyes cannot open when they should, so it is essential to watch a Shar Pei puppy's eyes carefully, especially during the early weeks and months of its life. Should there be any sign of discharge, blinking or other discomfort, a vet should be consulted without delay.

In severe cases, corrective surgery is necessary but often the problem can be rectified by eye tacking. This involves rolling out the eyelid and suturing it in place for a couple of weeks or so, allowing time for the wrinkles to smooth out. The procedure may need to be repeated as the puppy develops and wrinkles change.

ECTROPION
Ectropion is the reverse of entropion; occasionally, a dog can be affected by one in one eye and another in the other. Artificial tears can be helpful in the case of ectropion, for because the eyelids droop, or roll away from the eye, the conjunctiva is exposed, providing the eye with insufficient protection.

ULCERS IN THE EYE
Several breeds of dog can suffer from ulcers in the eye, so the Shar Pei is by no means alone in this field. They can be caused by injury, or by dust and debris entering the eye. This can happen whether or not a dog has entropion. At the first sign of trouble a vet should be contacted so that correct medication can be administered. The eye must, of course, be kept clean, and gentle bathing with warm water will help. Artificial tears, available

If you start out with a healthy Shar Pei from a reputable breeder, regardless of the puppy's colour, your chances of having a long-lived dog are quite promising.

from a vet or chemist, can also be beneficial to keep the eye lubricated.

TIGHT LIP
In cases when the padding on the lower lip of a Shar Pei is excessive, the lower lip can roll upward and then over the lower teeth. This makes it virtually impossible to expose the bite and causes two problems. There is the obvious discomfort suffered by the dog when chewing food, and in time the pressure placed on the lower teeth can push them backward, creating an overshot bite. Such dogs should of course never be used in a breeding programme, though corrective surgery can help them to live more comfortable lives.

ELONGATION OF THE SOFT PALATE
Elongation of the soft palate is not unusual in many of the shorter-nosed breeds and Shar Pei are no exception. Slight elongation causes few problems other than a tendency to snore. However, in worst cases, breathing and eating can be affected and a dog can tire easily, in which case veterinary attention is necessary to remove the excess tissue.

STENOTIC NARES
When a puppy inhales, the nostrils are compressed, causing closure of the air passages. Corrective surgery is necessary to remove part of the nose or nostril, and it goes without saying that no affected stock should ever be bred from.

EAR INFECTION
Because the Shar Pei's ears and ear canals are small, bacteria are quite likely to build up and cause infection. It is essential to check regularly for any sign of a waxy build up or unpleasant odour. Ear cleaning fluids are readily available, but one must never probe too deeply inside the ear. An affected ear causes substantial discomfort, often the head being constantly shaken and, in bad cases, held at an angle.

SKIN PROBLEMS
The Shar Pei is a breed that has a tendency to suffer from skin problems, caused in part by the wrinkled skin. There can also be soreness between the toes and

> **SKIN PROBLEMS**
> Eczema and dermatitis are skin problems that occur in many breeds and they can often be tricky problems to solve. Frequent bathing of the dog will remove skin oils and will cause the problem to worsen. Allergies to food or something in the environment can also cause the problem. Consider trying homeopathic remedies in addition to seeing your vet for direction.

Characteristics

> **KEEP AWAY FROM HEAT**
> A hot-blooded dog, no Shar Pei should be permitted to sit in the sun for long periods, nor should he sit too close to a fire or radiator. Heat can cause a Shar Pei to scratch and to moult. Sulphur tablets are a useful remedy to give when the body overheats.

inside the pads of the feet. Use of a medicated powder will help, and all dogs should be kept away from damp surfaces. Dogs should be prevented from chewing or licking at their feet, something that can sometimes happen as a result of boredom.

SHAR PEI RASH

Shar Pei rash is sometimes also called Shar Pei syndrome. Skin becomes red and inflamed and hair loss occurs in patches, giving a rather 'moth-eaten' appearance. It is believed that this may be due to the dog's own prickly hair, irritating its skin. Occasionally hair loss can affect the entire body, but unfortunately the symptoms do not respond well to treatment.

MUCINOSIS

This disorder is manifested by lumps and bumps on the skin, as well as possible discharge, caused by a mucous-like secretion forming under the skin.

Shar Pei tend to have more mucin than other dogs, accounting in part for the breed's plentiful wrinkles. Mucinosis is not a health concern, *per se,* though it does affect the appearance of the dog. If a dog develops an infection from mucinosis, antibiotics can be helpful.

RECTAL PROLAPSE

Rectal prolapse should never be confused with an anal abscess. This does occasionally happen in the Shar Pei, the prolapse occurring as an inflamed mass protruding from the anus. Blood may also be evident. There can be a number of different reasons for such prolapse, and veterinary attention should be sought urgently.

IMMUNE DEFICIENCY

Some Shar Pei lines carry immune deficiency, in which the immune system is depressed, though this sometimes seems to

Because the Shar Pei's ears are tiny, owners should check them regularly for waxy build-up or infection, taking care not to probe too deeply.

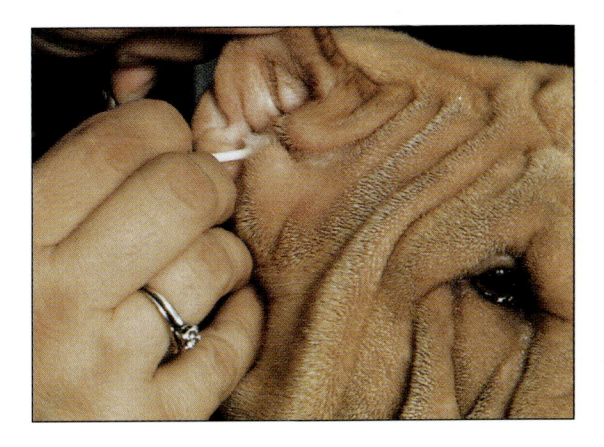

recover of its own accord as a puppy matures. This is frequently detected by a puppy having a high fever, with no apparent reason. There can be serious health problems in severe cases, and dogs so affected tend to be susceptible to demodectic mange.

HIP AND ELBOW DYSPLASIA
Hip dysplasia (HD) affects many different breeds of dog, the head of the femur not fitting neatly into the hip socket. This can cause continuous pressure on the joint, resulting in calcium deposits being formed. Arthritis can also result. A vet suspecting HD will guide an owner regarding the testing facilities now available, but a Shar Pei with badly affected hips should not be used for breeding.

Elbow dysplasia, a series of disorders that affect the elbow, has also been detected in the Shar Pei, usually being noticed between four and seven months of age.

Before acquiring your Shar Pei, you should discuss the various health concerns known in the breed with your chosen breeder. Regardless of any minor physical imperfection, your Shar Pei should be healthy and affectionate.

DO YOU KNOW ABOUT HIP DYSPLASIA?

Hip dysplasia is a fairly common condition found in purebred dogs. When a dog has hip dysplasia, its hind leg has an incorrectly formed hip joint. By constant use of the hip joint, it becomes more and more loose, wears abnormally and may become arthritic.

Hip dysplasia can only be confirmed with an x-ray, but certain symptoms may indicate a problem. Your dog may have a hip dysplasia problem if it walks in a peculiar manner, hops instead of smoothly runs, uses his hind legs in unison (to keep the pressure off the weak joint), has trouble getting up from a prone position or always sits with both legs together on one side of its body.

As the dog matures, it may adapt well to life with a bad hip, but in a few years the arthritis develops and many dogs with hip dysplasia become cripples.

Hip dysplasia is considered an inherited disease and only can be diagnosed definitively when the dog is two years old. Some experts claim that a special diet might help your puppy outgrow the bad hip, but the usual treatments are surgical. The removal of the pectineus muscle, the removal of the round part of the femur, reconstructing the pelvis and replacing the hip with an artificial one are all surgical interventions that are expensive, but they are usually very successful. Follow the advice of your veterinary surgeon.

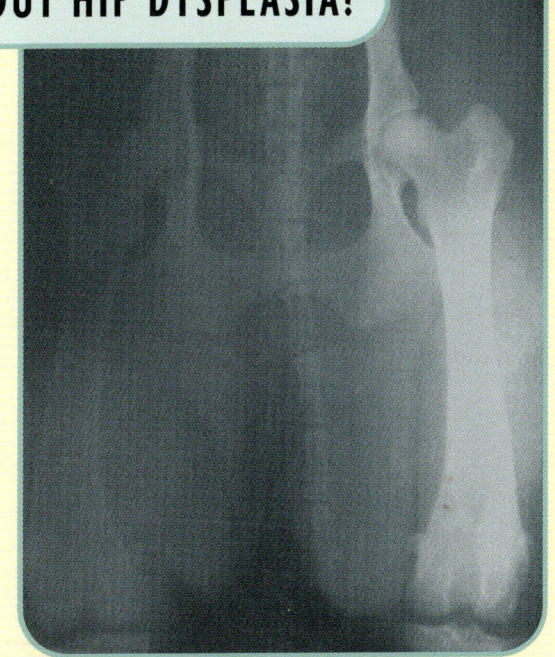

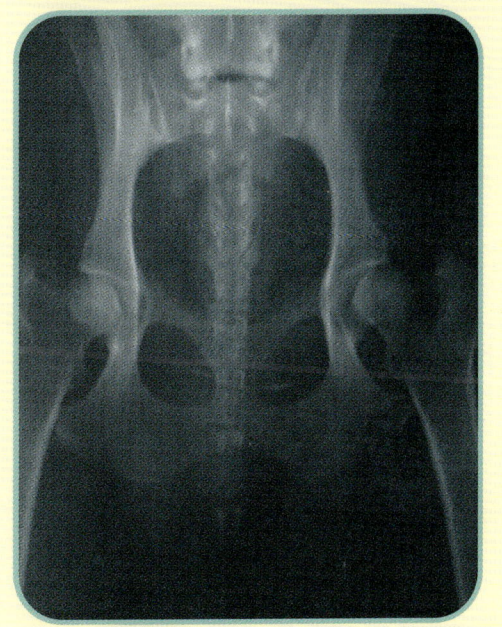

X-ray of a dog with 'Good' hips.

X-ray of a dog with 'Moderate' dysplastic hips.

The Breed Standard for the SHAR PEI

The breed standard of the Shar Pei is effectively designed to give a picture of the breed in words, rather than pictures. Indeed, the words are intended to create a visual picture in one's mind. Having said that, each person will probably interpret the words slightly differently, and reading a standard without having looked at good, typical representatives of the breed is never enough.

In addition, the standards vary slightly from country to country, so that when judging,

The breed standard is designed to provide a word picture of the ideal Shar Pei. These two Shar Pei have been evaluated on how well they conform to the standard. This is the basis of every dog show.

Breed Standard

The Shar Pei's head is rather large, with a flat skull and a moderately long and broad muzzle.

one should always aim to assess the dogs in relation to the standard of their own country. As years pass, standards are amended and updated, usually when the country's Kennel Club takes into consideration opinions expressed by breed clubs.

In Britain each standard commences with a short section under the heading 'General Appearance,' and this gives a short précis of what the Shar Pei should look like. You can see immediately that one is looking for a short-coupled, squarely built dog, so it is clearly evident that if a Shar Pei had a long body, it would be untypical.

In the knowledge that entropion has been a problem in this breed, The Kennel Club has actually incorporated the requirement that eyes should be free from entropion, explaining that the eyeball and lid should not be disturbed by skin, folds or hair. Such inclusions are highly valuable in engendering stability and good health within the breed.

In the Shar Pei standard the head and mouth are described in some detail, for both these aspects of the dog are unusual and need as much clarification as possible. Each other major section of the Shar Pei's anatomy, its temperament, its coat and colour are described, as is height, but the standard does

Because eye diseases are fairly common in Shar Pei, these potential problems are described in The Kennel Club standard. This is a unique feature of the Shar Pei breed standard.

The standard calls for an alert, active, short-coupled, squarely built dog.

not indicate any preferable weight. However, reading through the standard we notice words like 'powerful,' 'muscular,' 'strong.' So we can see that taking the standard as a whole, a picture of the breed is created.

However well one thinks one knows a breed, it is always worthwhile re-reading the breed standard from time to time. It is all too easy for breeders to conveniently overlook faults in their own stock, so turning back occasionally to the 'blueprint' of the breed helps to keep things in perspective. After all, we all strive to breed dogs that are a credit to their breed.

THE KENNEL CLUB STANDARD FOR THE SHAR PEI

General Appearance: Alert, active, compact, short-coupled, squarely built. Dogs larger and more powerful than bitches.

Characteristics: Loose skin, frowning expression.

Temperament: Calm, independent, very affectionate, and devoted to people.

Head and Skull: Rather large in proportion to body, skull flat, broad, moderate stop. Fine wrinkles on forehead and cheeks continuing to form dewlaps. Muzzle distinctive feature of breed; moderately long, broad from eyes to point of nose without any suggestion of tapering. Lips and top of muzzle well padded causing slight bulge at base of nose. When viewed from front, bottom jaw appears wider than top due to padding of lips. Nose large, wide, preferably black but any colour conforming to general coat colour permissible.

Eyes: Dark, medium size, almond-shaped with frowning expression. Lighter colour permissible in cream and light fawn dogs. Function of eyeball or lid in no way disturbed by surrounding skin, folds or hair. Any sign of irritation of eyeball, conjunctiva or eyelids highly undesirable. Free from entropion.

Ears: Very small, rather thick, equilaterally triangular in shape, slightly rounded at tip, with tips pointing towards eyes, set well forward over eyes, wide apart and close to skull. Pricked ears highly undesirable.

The desired ears are very small and thick, appearing as equilateral triangles.

Mouth: Bluish-black tongue preferred, pink-spotted permissible. Solid pink tongue undesir-

The bluish-black tongue is a preferred characteristic of the breed.

Judges at a dog show should check the Shar Pei's tongue to make sure that it is of the desired bluish-black coloration.

The Shar Pei's ears are shaped like equilateral (equal-sided) triangles with rounded ends.

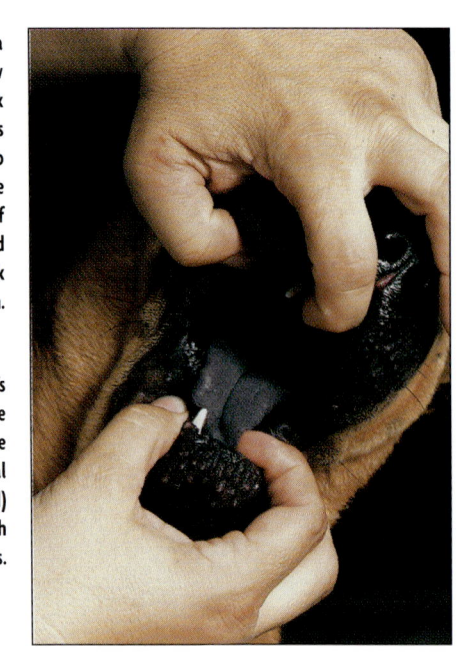

able. Flews, roof of mouth and gums preferably black, lighter colours permissible in cream and light fawn. Teeth strong, with a perfect, regular and complete scissor bite, i.e. upper teeth closely overlapping lower teeth and set square to the jaws. Padding of lower lips should not be so excessive as to interfere with the bite.

The lips are padded but not excessively so as to interfere with the dog's bite. The teeth meet in a scissor bite.

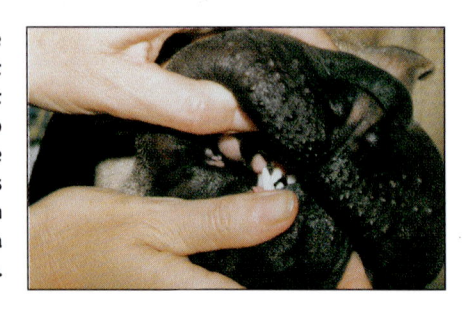

Neck: Short, strong, full; set well on shoulders, with loose skin under neck.

Forequarters: Shoulders muscular, well laid and sloping. Forelegs straight, moderate length, good bone; pasterns slightly sloping, strong and flexible.

Body: Chest broad and deep, underline rising slightly under loin; back short, strong; topline dips slightly behind withers then rises over short, broad loin. Excessive skin on body when mature highly undesirable.

Hindquarters: Muscular, strong; moderately angulated; hocks well let down.

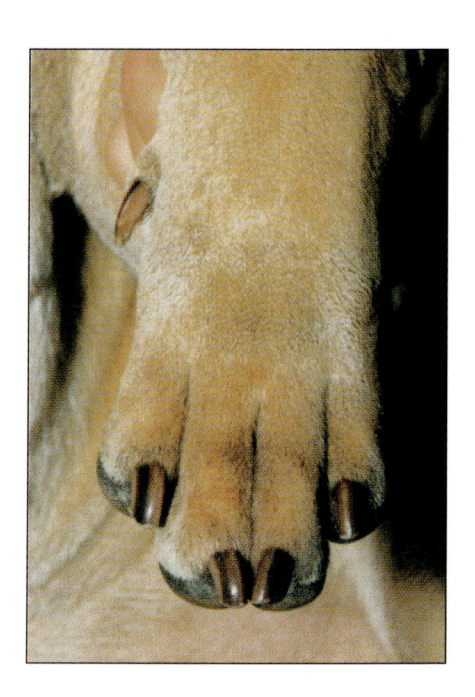

Breed Standard

Gait/Movement: Free, balanced, vigorous.

Coat: Distinctive feature of breed. Short and bristly; harsh to touch. Straight and off-standing on body, generally flatter on

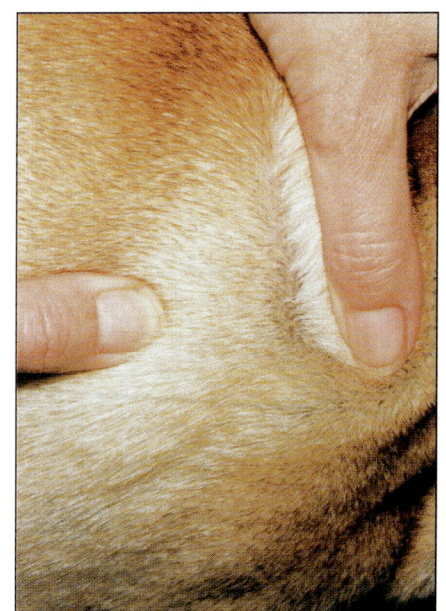

Well-formed foot with well-pedicured toenails.

Typical coat texture of the Shar Pei, short and bristly, standing off from body.

Feet: Moderate size, compact, toes well knuckled. Fore and hind dewclaws may be removed.

Tail: Rounded, narrowing to fine point, base set very high. May be carried high and curved, carried in tight curl, or curved over. Lack of tail highly undesirable.

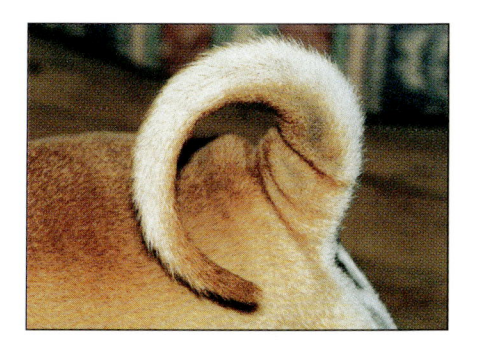

HONG KONG STANDARD
The Hong Kong standard for the Shar Pei includes detailed descriptions of the various breed colours, including solids in black, fawn, red, cream and dilute ('hot cream'), rust and chocolate. The standard indicates that solid colours are the only colours desired, disqualifying dogs that are particoloured, black and tan or brindle.

The tail should be rounded and narrowing to a fine point, like this one. The length of coat on the tail is a good indication of overall coat length and texture.

A POETIC TRANSLATION OF THE ORIGINAL BREED STANDARD

California breeder Joseph Chan translated the original Chinese standard, which is most poetic in its description of the Shar Pei. The standard includes such details as *wu-lo* head (a pear-shaped melon), small clam shell ears, butterfly nose (not referring to coloration but to the shape of a cookie), *pae pah* legs (a ham-shaped musical instrument), shrimp back, iron-wire tail, grandma face (properly wrinkled), iron pellet tongue (the bluish-black colour), water buffalo neck, wun fish body (not too round or flat), facing sky anus, horse's rear end, dragon leg, garlic bulb feet and a mother frog mouth.

limbs. No undercoat. Over 2.5 cms (1 in) long undesirable. Never trimmed.

Colour: Solid colours—black, red, light or dark shades of fawn and cream. Frequently shaded on tail and back of thighs with lighter colour; patched white or spotted undesirable.

Size: Height: 46–51 cms (18–20 ins) at withers.

Faults: Any departure from the foregoing points should be considered a fault and the seriousness with which the fault should be regarded should be in exact proportion to its degree.

Note: Male animals should have two apparently normal testicles fully descended into the scrotum.

Free, balanced and vigorous gait is an important feature of the Shar Pei.

Breed Standard   **37**

Above all, the Shar Pei must be an intelligent, friendly dog with a deep devotion to people.

Your Puppy
SHAR PEI

'LET'S-GET-ACQUAINTED'
You should not even think about buying a puppy that looks sick, undernourished, overly frightened or nervous. Sometimes a timid puppy will warm up to you after a 30-minute 'let's-get-acquainted' session.

HOW TO SELECT A PUPPY
First and foremost, before selecting a puppy, it is essential to have decided that the Shar Pei is really the right breed for you and your family. You will have considered the size of the breed, its temperament and strength, and also the coat that can, occasionally, cause an allergic reaction. You must also be absolutely certain that funds are available for veterinary bills or pet insurance. You should bear in mind that although you hope your dog will live a healthy life, Shar Pei do encounter their fair share of health problems. If you have small children or elderly people in your household, you must carefully consider whether they can cope with a Shar Pei around the home, though where children are concerned, much will depend on sensible parental control.

All Shar Pei puppies look enchanting, but you must select one from a caring breeder who has given the puppies all the attention they have needed and has looked after them well. A young puppy should look well fed, but not pot-bellied, as this might indicate worms. Take a note of eyes that should look bright and clear, without discharge. Nor, of course, should there be any discharge from the nose and certainly no evidence of loose motions.

Check the coat carefully, too. There should be no sign of a rash and no bare patches. A Shar Pei should have an alert personality and should appear neither lethargic nor aggressive, either with people or with the other puppies. Take care also that you do not select a puppy that is excessively shy.

WHERE TO BEGIN?
If you are convinced that the Shar Pei is the ideal dog for you, it's time to learn about where to find a puppy and what to look for. Locating a litter of Shar Pei should not be too terribly difficult for the new owner. You should enquire about breeders who enjoy a good reputation in the breed. You are looking for an experienced breeder with outstanding dog ethics and a strong commitment to the breed. New owners should have as many questions as they have doubts. An experienced breeder is indeed the one to answer all of your questions and help you determine if your choice of the Shar Pei is a good one. An experienced breeder will sell you a puppy at a fair price if,

PREPARING FOR PUP
Unfortunately, when a puppy is bought by someone who does not take into consideration the time and attention that dog ownership requires, it is the puppy who suffers when he is either abandoned or placed in a shelter by a frustrated owner. So all of the 'homework' you do in preparation for your pup's arrival will benefit you both. The more informed you are, the more you will know what to expect and the better equipped you will be to handle the ups and downs of raising a puppy. Hopefully, everyone in the household is willing to do his part in raising and caring for the pup. The anticipation of owning a dog often brings a lot of promises from excited family members: 'I will walk him every day,' 'I will feed him,' 'I will housebreak him,' etc., but these things take time and effort, and promises can easily be forgotten once the novelty of the new pet has worn off.

Like all puppies, Shar Pei puppies are curious and playful. This well-wrinkled trio appears ready for a bit of mischief.

and only if, the breeder determines that you are a suitable, worthy owner of his dogs. An experienced breeder can be relied upon for advice, no matter what time of day or night. A reputable breeder will accept a puppy back, without questions, should you decide that this is not the right dog for you.

SELECTING A BREEDER
When choosing a breeder, reputation is much more important than convenience of location. Do not be overly impressed by breeders who run brag advertisements in the dog presses about their 'proven stock.' The real quality breeders are quiet and unassuming. You hear about them at shows, by word of mouth. These breeders have extended dog families, clients who have become happy Shar Pei devotees who live with their dogs and keep in touch to report the dogs' growth and accomplishments.

While health considerations in the Shar Pei are extremely important in this breed, socialisation is of great importance. Since the Shar Pei's temperament can vary from line to line, socialisation is the first and best way to encourage a proper, stable personality. Breeders have successfully rid lines of nasty temperaments as well as aggressive tendencies, but it's wise for owners to be aware.

Although The Kennel Club will be able to put you in contact with a breed club, or perhaps directly with breeders, you must select a breeder with the utmost care. Initially it is always a good idea to visit a large show at which Shar Pei will be exhibited. Here you will have an opportunity to meet various breeders, to see the quality of their own stock and to observe the care the Shar-Pei have been given.

A VISIT TO THE LITTER

Now that you have contacted and met a breeder or two and made your choice about which breeder is best suited to your needs, it's time to visit the litter. Keep in mind that many top breeders have waiting lists. Sometimes new owners have to wait as long as two years for a puppy. If you are really committed to the breeder whom you've selected, then you will wait (and hope for an early arrival!). If not, you may have to resort to your second or third

DOCUMENTATION

Two important documents you will get from the breeder are the pup's pedigree and registration certificate. The breeder should register the litter and each pup with The Kennel Club, and it is necessary for you to have the paperwork if you plan on showing or breeding in the future.

Make sure you know the breeder's intentions on which type of registration he will obtain for the pup. There are limited registrations which may prohibit the dog from being shown, bred or from competing in non-conformation trials such as Working or Agility if the breeder feels that the pup is not of sufficient quality to do so. There is also a type of registration that will permit the dog in non-conformation competition only.

On the reverse side of the registration certificate, the new owner can find the transfer section which must be signed by the breeder.

INSURANCE

Many good breeders will offer you insurance with your new puppy, which is an excellent idea. The first few weeks of insurance will probably be covered free of charge or with only minimal cost, allowing you to take up the policy when this expires. If you own a pet dog, it is sensible to take out such a policy as veterinary fees can be high, although routine vaccinations and boosters are not covered. Look carefully at the many options open to you before deciding which suits you best.

PUPPY SELECTION

Your selection of a good puppy can be determined by your needs. A show potential or a good pet? It is your choice. Every puppy, however, should be of good temperament. Although show-quality puppies are bred and raised with emphasis on physical conformation, responsible breeders strive for equally good temperament. Do not buy from a breeder who concentrates solely on physical beauty at the expense of personality.

choice breeder. Don't be too anxious, however. If the breeder doesn't have a waiting list, or any customers, there is probably a good reason. It's no different than visiting a pub with no clientele. The better pubs and restaurants always have a waiting list—and it's usually worth the wait. Besides, isn't a puppy more important than a pint?

Since you are likely to be choosing a Shar Pei as a pet dog and not a show dog, you simply should select a pup that is friendly and attractive. Shar Pei generally have medium-sized litters, averaging four to five puppies, and many litters present quite a rainbow of colour selection to the potential buyer. Be colour blind: select for temperament, health and structure. Be wary of the shy or overly aggressive puppy; be especially conscious of the nervous Shar Pei pup. Don't let sentiment or emotion trap you into buying the runt of the litter.

Breeders commonly allow visitors to see the litter by around the fifth or sixth week, and puppies leave for their new homes between the eighth and tenth week. Breeders who permit their puppies to leave early are more interested in your pounds than their puppies' well being. Puppies need to learn the rules of the pack from their dams, and most dams continue teaching the pups manners and dos and don'ts until around the eighth week. Breeders spend significant amounts of time with the Shar Pei toddlers so that they are able to interact with the 'other species,' i.e. humans. Given the long history that dogs and humans have, bonding between the two species is natural but must be nurtured.

Always check the bite of your selected puppy to be sure that it is neither overshot nor undershot. This may not be too noticeable on a young puppy but it is a fairly common problem with certain lines of Shar Pei. Check also to see that the puppy's mouth is not excessively padded, thereby interfering with the pup's bite. Of course, check the eyes and skin carefully, since in the Shar Pei, these are the most common areas of health problems.

COMMITMENT OF OWNERSHIP

After considering all of these factors, you have most likely

ARE YOU A FIT OWNER?
If the breeder from whom you are buying a puppy asks you a lot of personal questions, do not be insulted. Such a breeder wants to be sure that you will be a fit provider for his puppy.

PUPPY APPEARANCE
Your puppy should have a well-fed appearance but not a distended abdomen, which may indicate worms or incorrect feeding, or both. The body should be firm, with a solid feel. The skin of the abdomen should be pale pink and clean, without signs of scratching or rash. Check the hind legs to make certain that dewclaws were removed, if any were present at birth.

already made some very important decisions about selecting your puppy. You have chosen a Shar Pei, which means that you have decided which characteristics you want in a

Breeders rarely allow visitors when the litter is this young, so this photograph is an exciting peek at a Shar Pei litter in its first week of life.

dog and what type of dog will best fit into your family and lifestyle. If you have selected a breeder, you have gone a step further—you have done your research and found a responsible, conscientious person who breeds quality Shar Pei and who should be a reliable source of help as you and your puppy adjust to life together. If you have observed a litter in action, you have obtained a firsthand look at the dynamics of a puppy 'pack' and, thus, you should learn about each pup's individual personality—perhaps you have even found one that particularly appeals to you.

However, even if you have not yet found the Shar Pei puppy of your dreams, observing pups will help you learn to recognise certain behaviour and to determine what a pup's behaviour indicates about his temperament. You will be able to pick out which pups are the leaders, which ones are less outgoing, which ones are confident, which ones are shy, playful, friendly, aggressive, etc. Equally as important, you will learn to recognise what a healthy pup should look and act like. All of these things will help you in your search, and when you find the Shar Pei that was meant for you, you will know it!

Researching your breed, selecting a responsible breeder and observing as many pups as possible are all important steps on the way to dog ownership. It may seem like a lot of effort…and you have not even taken the pup home yet! Remember, though, you cannot be too careful when it comes to deciding on the type of dog you want and finding out about your

DID YOU KNOW?

Breeders rarely release puppies until they are eight to ten weeks of age. This is an acceptable age for most breeds of dog, excepting toy breeds, which are not released until around 12 weeks, given their petite sizes. If a breeder has a puppy that is 12 weeks or more, it is likely well socialised and housetrained. Be sure that it is otherwise healthy before deciding to take it home.

prospective pup's background. Buying a puppy is not—or should not be—just another whimsical purchase. This is one instance in which you actually do get to choose your own family! You may be thinking that buying a puppy should be fun—it should not be so serious and so much work. Keep in mind that your puppy is not a cuddly stuffed toy or decorative lawn ornament, but a creature that will become a real member of your family. You will come to realise that, while buying a puppy is a pleasurable and exciting endeavour, it is not something to be taken lightly. Relax…the fun will start when the pup comes home!

Always keep in mind that a puppy is nothing more than a baby in a furry disguise…a baby who is virtually helpless in a human world and who trusts his owner for fulfilment of his basic needs for survival. In addition to water and shelter, your pup needs care, protection, guidance and love. If you are not prepared to commit to this, then you are not prepared to own a dog.

Wait a minute, you say. How hard could this be? All of my neighbours own dogs and they seem to be doing just fine. Why should I have to worry about all of this? Well, you should not worry about it; in fact, you will

> **YOUR SCHEDULE . . .**
> If you lead an erratic, unpredictable life, with daily or weekly changes in your work requirements, consider the problems of owning a puppy. The new puppy has to be fed regularly, socialised (loved, petted, handled, introduced to other people) and, most importantly, allowed to visit outdoors for toilet training. As the dog gets older, it can be more tolerant of deviations in its feeding and toilet relief.

probably find that once your Shar Pei pup gets used to his new home, he will fall into his place in the family quite naturally. But it never hurts to emphasise the commitment of dog ownership. With some time and patience, it is really not too difficult to raise a curious and exuberant Shar Pei pup to be a well-adjusted and well-mannered adult dog—a dog that could be your most loyal friend.

PREPARING PUPPY'S PLACE IN YOUR HOME
Researching your breed and finding a breeder are only two aspects of the 'homework' you will have to do before taking your Shar Pei puppy home. You will also have to prepare your home and family for the new addition. Much as you would prepare a nursery for a newborn baby, you will need to designate a place in your home that will be the puppy's own. How you prepare your home will depend on how much freedom the dog will be allowed. Whatever you decide, you must ensure that he has a place that he can 'call his own.'

When you bring your new puppy into your home, you are bringing him into what will become his home as well. Obviously, you did not buy a puppy so that he could take over your house, but in order for a puppy to grow into a stable, well-adjusted dog, he has to feel comfortable in his surroundings.

Your new Shar Pei puppy should retire to its own bed or crate, instead of snuggling in bed with you!

Your Puppy

47

> **QUALITY FOOD**
> The cost of food must also be mentioned. All dogs need a good quality food with an adequate supply of protein to develop their bones and muscles properly. Most dogs are not picky eaters but unless fed properly they can quickly succumb to skin problems.

Remember, he is leaving the warmth and security of his mother and littermates, as well as the familiarity of the only place he has ever known, so it is important to make his transition as easy as possible. By preparing a place in your home for the puppy, you are making him feel as welcome as possible in a strange new place. It should not take him long to get used to it, but the sudden shock of being transplanted is somewhat traumatic for a young pup. Imagine how a small child would feel in the same situation—that is how your puppy must be feeling. It is up to you to reassure him and to let him know, 'Little chap, you are going to like it here!'

WHAT YOU SHOULD BUY

CRATE
To someone unfamiliar with the use of crates in dog training, it may seem like punishment to shut a dog in a crate, but this is not the case at all. Although all breeders do not advocate crate training, more and more breeders and trainers are recommending crates as a preferred tool for show puppies as well as pet puppies. Crates are not cruel—crates have many humane and highly effective uses in dog care and training. For example, crate training is a very popular and very successful housebreaking method. A crate can keep your dog safe during travel and, perhaps most importantly, a crate provides your dog with a place of his own in your home. It serves as a 'doggie bedroom' of sorts—your Shar Pei can curl up in his crate when he wants to sleep or when he just needs a break. Many dogs sleep in their crates overnight. With soft bedding and his favourite toy, a

> **FEEDING TIP**
> You will probably start feeding your pup the same food that he has been getting from the breeder; the breeder should give you a few days' supply to start you off. Although you should not give your pup too many treats, you will want to have puppy treats on hand for coaxing, training, rewards, etc. Be careful, though, as a small pup's calorie requirements are relatively low and a few treats can add up to almost a full day's worth of calories without the required nutrition.

you. It will most likely be one of the two most popular types: wire or fibreglass. There are advantages and disadvantages to each type. For example, a wire crate is more open, allowing the air to flow through and affording the dog a view of what is going on around him while a fibreglass crate is sturdier. Both can double as travel crates, providing protection for the dog. The size of the crate is another thing to consider. Puppies do not stay puppies forever—in fact, sometimes it seems as if they grow right before your eyes. A small crate may be fine for a very young Shar Pei pup, but it will not do him much good for long! Unless you have the money and the inclination to buy a new crate every time your pup has a growth spurt, it is better to get one that will accommodate your dog both as a pup and at full size. A medium-size crate will be necessary for a full-grown Shar Pei, who stands approximately 20 inches high.

BEDDING
Veterinary bedding in the dog's crate will help the dog feel more at home and you may also like to pop in a small blanket. This will take the place of the leaves, twigs, etc., that the pup would use in the wild to make a den; the pup can make his own 'burrow' in the crate. Although

Your local pet shop should have a wide selection of crates from which you can select an appropriate one for your Shar Pei.

crate becomes a cosy pseudo-den for your dog. Like his ancestors, he too will seek out the comfort and retreat of a den—you just happen to be providing him with something a little more luxurious than what his early ancestors enjoyed.

As far as purchasing a crate, the type that you buy is up to

Your Puppy

49

your pup is far removed from his den-making ancestors, the denning instinct is still a part of his genetic makeup. Second, until you take your pup home, he has been sleeping amidst the warmth of his mother and littermates, and while a blanket is not the same as a warm, breathing body, it still provides heat and something with which to snuggle. You will want to wash your pup's bedding frequently in case he has an accident in his crate, and replace or remove any blanket that becomes ragged and starts to fall apart.

Toys

Toys are a must for dogs of all ages, especially for curious playful pups. Puppies are the 'children' of the dog world, and what child does not love toys? Chew toys provide enjoyment for both dog and owner—your dog will enjoy playing with his favourite toys, while you will enjoy the fact that they distract him from your expensive shoes

CRATE TRAINING TIPS

During crate training, you should partition off the section of the crate in which the pup stays. If he is given too big an area, this will hinder your training efforts. Crate training is based on the fact that a dog does not like to soil his sleeping quarters, so it is ineffective to keep a pup in a crate that is so big that he can eliminate in one end and get far enough away from it to sleep. Also, you want to make the crate den-like for the pup. Blankets and a favourite toy will make the crate cosy for the small pup; as he grows, you may want to evict some of his 'roommates' to make more room.

It will take some coaxing at first, but be patient. Given some time to get used to it, your pup will adapt to his new home-within-a-home quite nicely.

Get a crate that will be large enough to hold your Shar Pei when it reaches full size.

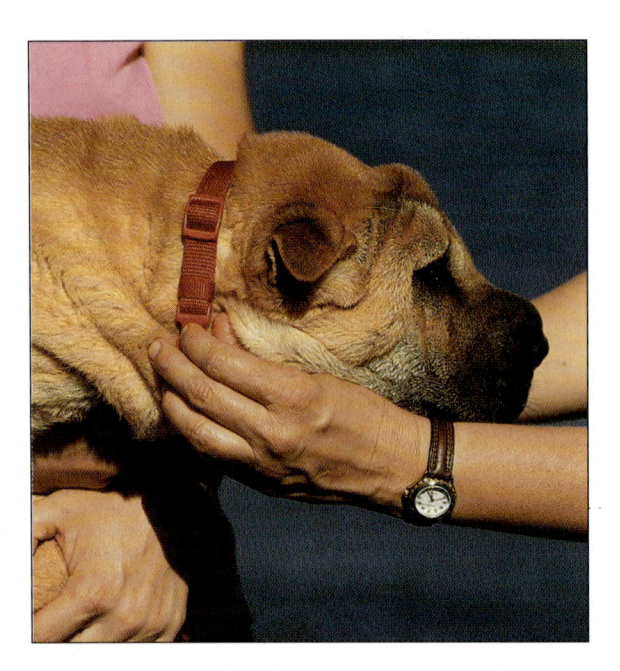

A nylon collar is a good choice for your Shar Pei. It is lightweight, yet sturdy, and can be adjusted in size as the dog grows.

and leather sofa. Puppies love to chew; in fact, chewing is a physical need for pups as they are teething, and everything looks appetising! The full range of your possessions—from old tea towel to Oriental carpet—are fair game in the eyes of a teething pup. Puppies are not all that discerning when it comes to finding something to literally 'sink their teeth into'— everything tastes great!

Shar Pei puppies are not terribly aggressive chewers, but they do enjoy nylon bones. Only safe toys should be offered to them, and owners should always monitor a dog who is playing with soft, fluffy toys, which tend to be Shar Pei's favourites. Be sure that the Shar Pei doesn't de-stuff his little fluffy friends and attempt to eat the filling.

Squeaky toys are quite popular, but must be avoided for the Shar Pei. Perhaps a squeaky toy can be used as an aid in training, but not for free play. If a pup 'disembowels' one of these, the small plastic squeaker inside can be dangerous if swallowed. Monitor the condition of all your pup's toys carefully and get rid of any that have been chewed to the point of becoming potentially dangerous.

Be careful of natural bones, which have a tendency to splinter into sharp, dangerous pieces. Also be careful of rawhide, which can turn into pieces that are easy to swallow and become a mushy mess on your carpet.

Lead

A nylon lead is probably the best option as it is the most resistant to puppy teeth should your pup take a liking to chewing on his lead. Of course, this is a habit that should be nipped in the bud, but if your pup likes to chew on his lead he has a very slim chance of being able to chew through the strong nylon. Nylon leads are also lightweight, which is good for a young Shar Pei who is just

Your Puppy

getting used to the idea of walking on a lead. For everyday walking and safety purposes, the nylon lead is a good choice. As your pup grows up and gets used to walking on the lead, you may want to purchase a flexible lead. These leads allow you to extend the length to give the dog a broader area to explore or to shorten the length to keep the dog near you. Of course there are special leads for training purposes, and specially made leather harnesses, but these are not necessary for routine walks.

COLLAR

Your pup should get used to wearing a collar all the time

TOYS, TOYS, TOYS!

With a big variety of dog toys available, and so many that look like they would be a lot of fun for a dog, be careful in your selection. It is amazing what a set of puppy teeth can do to an innocent-looking toy, so, obviously, safety is a major consideration. Be sure to choose the most durable products that you can find. Hard nylon bones and toys are a safe bet, and many of them are offered in different scents and flavours that will be sure to capture your dog's attention. It is always fun to play a game of catch with your dog, and there are balls and flying discs that are specially made to withstand dog teeth.

Select a lightweight lead to begin training your Shar Pei.

CHOOSE AN APPROPRIATE COLLAR

The BUCKLE COLLAR is the standard collar used for everyday purpose. Be sure that you adjust the buckle on growing puppies. Check it every day. It can become too tight overnight! These collars can be made of leather or nylon. Attach your dog's identification tags to this collar.

The CHOKE COLLAR is the usual collar recommended for training. It is constructed of highly polished steel so that it slides easily through the stainless steel loop. The idea is that the dog controls the pressure around its neck and he will stop pulling if the collar becomes uncomfortable. Never leave a choke collar on your dog when not training.

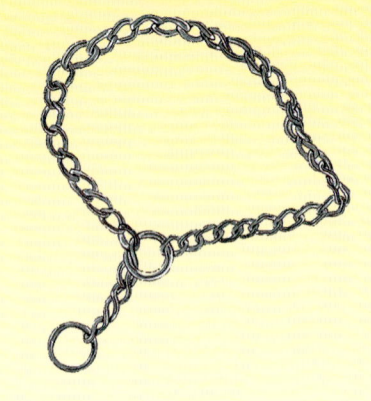

The HALTER is for a trained dog that has to be restrained to prevent running away, chasing a cat and the like. Considered the most humane of all collars, it is frequently used on smaller dogs for which collars are not comfortable.

Your Puppy

since you will want to attach his ID tags to it. You have to attach the lead to something! A lightweight nylon collar is a good choice; make sure that it fits snugly enough so that the pup cannot wriggle out of it, but is loose enough so that it will not be uncomfortably tight around the pup's neck. You should be able to fit a finger between the pup and the collar. It may take some time for your pup to get used to wearing the collar, but soon he will not even notice that it is there. Choke collars are made for training, but should only be used by an experienced handler. Some breeders recommend head collars, which fit over the dog's head, as the preferred device to train a Shar Pei.

MENTAL AND DENTAL
Toys not only help your puppy get the physical and mental stimulation he needs but also provide a great way to keep his teeth clean. Hard rubber or nylon toys, especially those constructed with grooves, are designed to scrape away plaque, preventing bad breath and gum infection.

FINANCIAL RESPONSIBILITY
Grooming tools, collars, leashes, dog beds and, of course, toys will be an expense to you when you first obtain your pup, and the cost will continue throughout your dog's lifetime. If your puppy damages or destroys your possessions (as most puppies surely will!) or something belonging to a neighbour, you can calculate additional expense. There is also flea and pest control, which every dog owner faces more than once. You must be able to handle the financial responsibility of owning a dog.

FOOD AND WATER BOWLS
Your pup will need two bowls, one for food and one for water. You may want two sets of bowls, one for inside and one for outside, depending on where the dog will be fed and where he will be spending time. Stainless steel or sturdy plastic bowls are popular choices. Plastic bowls are more chewable. Dogs tend not to chew on the steel variety, which can be sterilised. It is important to buy sturdy bowls since anything is in danger of being

Your local pet shop sells an array of dishes and bowls for water and food.

chewed by puppy teeth and you do not want your dog to be constantly chewing apart his bowl (for his safety and for your purse!).

CLEANING SUPPLIES
Until a pup is housetrained you will be doing a lot of cleaning. Accidents will occur, which is acceptable in the beginning because the puppy does not know any better. All you can do is be prepared to clean up any 'accidents.' Old rags, towels, newspapers and a safe disinfectant are good to have on hand.

BEYOND THE BASICS
The items previously discussed are the bare necessities. You will find out what else you need as you go along—grooming supplies, flea/tick protection, baby gates to partition a room, etc. These things will vary depending on your situation but it is important that you have everything you need to feed and make your Shar Pei comfortable in his first few days at home.

PUPPY-PROOFING YOUR HOME
Aside from making sure that your Shar Pei will be comfortable in your home, you also have to make sure that your home is safe for your Shar Pei. This means taking precautions that your pup will not get into anything he should not get into

Your Puppy 55

and that there is nothing within his reach that may harm him should he sniff it, chew it, inspect it, etc. This probably seems obvious since, while you are primarily concerned with your pup's safety, at the same time you do not want your belongings to be ruined. Breakables should be placed out of reach if your dog is to have full run of the house. If he is to be limited to certain places within the house, keep any potentially dangerous items in the 'off-limits' areas. An electrical cord can pose a danger should the puppy decide to taste it—and who is going to convince a pup that it would not make a great chew toy? Cords should be fastened tightly against the wall. If your dog is going to spend time in a crate, make sure that there is nothing near his crate that he can reach if he sticks his curious little nose or paws through the openings. Just as you would with a child, keep all household

It is your responsibility to clean up after your dog. Your local pet shop will have various devices to make the job as convenient as possible.

NATURAL TOXINS
Examine your grass and garden landscaping before bringing your puppy home. Many varieties of plants have leaves, stems or flowers that are toxic if ingested, and you can depend on a curious puppy to investigate them. Ask your vet for information on poisonous plants or research them at your library.

CHEMICAL TOXINS

Scour your garage for potential puppy dangers. Remove weed killers, pesticides and antifreeze materials. Antifreeze is highly toxic and even a few drops can kill an adult dog. The sweet taste attracts the animal, who will quickly consume it from the floor or curbside.

cleaners and chemicals where the pup cannot reach them.

It is also important to make sure that the outside of your home is safe. Of course your puppy should never be unsupervised, but a pup let loose in the garden will want to run and explore, and he should be granted that freedom. Do not let a fence give you a false sense of security; you would be surprised how crafty (and persistent) a dog can be in working out how to dig under and squeeze his way through small holes, or to jump or climb over a fence. The remedy is to make the fence well embedded into the ground and high enough so that it really is impossible for your dog to get over it (about 3 metres should suffice). Be sure to repair or secure any gaps in the fence. Check the fence periodically to ensure that it is in good shape and make repairs as needed; a very determined pup may return to the same spot to 'work on it' until he is able to get through.

FIRST TRIP TO THE VET

You have selected your puppy, and your home and family are ready. Now all you have to do is collect your Shar Pei from the breeder and the fun begins, right? Well...not so fast. Something else you need to prepare is your pup's first trip to the veterinary surgeon. Perhaps the breeder can recommend someone in the area that specialises in Shar Pei, or maybe you know some other Shar Pei owners who can suggest a good vet. Either way, you should have an appointment arranged for your pup before you pick him up.

The pup's first visit will consist of an overall examination to make sure that the pup does not have any problems that are not apparent to the eye. The veterinary surgeon will also set up a schedule for the pup's

PUPPY-PROOFING

Thoroughly puppy-proof your house before bringing your puppy home. Never use roach or rodent poisons in any area accessible to the puppy. Avoid the use of toilet cleaners. Most dogs are born with 'toilet sonar' and will take a drink if the lid is left open. Also keep the rubbish secured and out of reach.

Your Puppy 57

Mischief-making can be a merry time for Shar Pei puppies. Owners must carefully monitor their pups in the home to make sure that they do not develop bad habits that can harm them.

Your rapport with your chosen veterinary surgeon is important. Perhaps a fellow Shar Pei owner or your breeder can recommend a good vet with experience in Shar Pei.

ride to your home is likely to be the first time he has been in a car. The last thing you want to do is smother him, as this will only frighten him further. This is not to say that human contact is not extremely necessary at this stage, because this is the time when a connection between the pup and his human family is formed. Gentle petting and soothing words should help console him, as well as just vaccinations; the breeder will inform you of which ones the pup has already received and the vet can continue from there.

INTRODUCTION TO THE FAMILY

Everyone in the house will be excited about the puppy coming home and will want to pet him and play with him, but it is best to make the introduction low-key so as not to overwhelm the puppy. He is apprehensive already. It is the first time he has been separated from his mother and the breeder, and the

A FORTNIGHT'S GRACE
It will take at least two weeks for your puppy to become accustomed to his new surroundings. Give him lots of love, attention, handling, frequent opportunities to relieve himself, a diet he likes to eat and a place he can call his own.

putting him down and letting him explore on his own (under your watchful eye, of course).

The pup may approach the family members or may busy himself with exploring for a while. Gradually, each person should spend some time with the pup, one at a time, crouching down to get as close to the pup's level as possible and letting him sniff their hands and petting him gently. He definitely needs human attention and he needs to be touched—this is how to form an immediate bond. Just remember that the pup is experiencing a lot of things for the first time, at the same time. There are new people, new noises, new smells, and new things to investigate: so be gentle, be affectionate, and be as comforting as you can be.

PUP'S FIRST NIGHT HOME
You have travelled home with your new charge safely in his crate. He's been to the vet for a thorough check-up; he's been weighed, his papers examined; perhaps he's even been vaccinated and wormed as well. He's met the family, licked the whole family, including the excited children and the less-than-happy cat. He's explored his area, his new bed, the garden and anywhere else he's been permitted. He's eaten his first meal at home and relieved

THE TRIP HOME
Taking your dog from the breeder to your home in a car can be a very uncomfortable experience for both of you. The puppy will have been taken from his warm, friendly, safe environment and brought into a strange new environment. An environment that moves! Be prepared for loose bowels, urination, crying, whining and even fear biting. With proper love and encouragement when you arrive home, the stress of the trip should quickly disappear.

A puppy shows its personality very early in life as it plays with its mother. An alert, playful puppy is a desirable puppy.

himself in the proper place. He's heard lots of new sounds, smelled new friends and seen more of the outside world than ever before.

That was just the first day! He's worn out and is ready for bed…or so you think!

It's puppy's first night and you are ready to say 'Good night'—keep in mind that this is puppy's first night ever to be sleeping alone. His dam and littermates are no longer at paw's length and he's a bit scared, cold and lonely. Be

PUPPY PERSONALITY
When a litter becomes available to you, choosing a pup out of all those adorable faces will not be an easy task! Sound temperament is of utmost importance, but each pup has its own personality and some may be better suited to you than others. A feisty, independent pup will do well in a home with older children and adults, while quiet, shy puppies will thrive in a home with minimum noise and distractions. Your breeder knows the pups best and should be able to guide you in the right direction.

reassuring to your new family member. This is not the time to spoil him and give in to his inevitable whining.

Puppies whine. They whine to let others know where they are and hopefully to get company out of it. Place your pup in his new bed or crate in his room and close the door. Mercifully, he may fall asleep without a peep. If the inevitable occurs, ignore the whining: he is fine. Be strong and keep his interest in mind. Do not allow yourself to feel guilty and visit the pup. He will fall asleep eventually.

Many breeders recommend placing a piece of bedding from his former home in his new bed so that he recognises the scent of his littermates. Others still advise placing a hot water bottle in his bed for warmth. This latter may be a good idea provided the pup doesn't attempt to suckle—he'll get good and wet and may not fall asleep so fast.

Puppy's first night can be somewhat stressful for the pup and his new family. Remember that you are setting the tone of nighttime at your house. Unless you want to play with your pup every evening at 10 p.m., midnight and 2 a.m., don't initiate the habit. Your family will thank you, and so will your pup!

PUPPY PROBLEMS

The majority of problems that are commonly seen in young pups will disappear as your dog gets older. However, how you deal with problems when he is young will determine how he reacts to discipline as an adult dog. It is important to establish who is boss (hopefully it will be you!) right away when you are first bonding with your dog. This bond will set the tone for the rest of your life together.

> **SOCIALISATION**
> Thorough socialisation includes not only meeting new people but also being introduced to new experiences such as riding in the car, having his coat brushed, hearing the television, walking in a crowd—the list is endless. The more your pup experiences, and the more positive the experiences are, the less of a shock and the less frightening it will be for your pup to encounter new things.

PREVENTING PUPPY PROBLEMS

SOCIALISATION

Now that you have done all of the preparatory work and have helped your pup get accustomed to his new home and family, it is about time for you to have some fun! Socialising your Shar Pei pup gives you the opportunity to show off your new friend, and your pup gets to reap the benefits of being an adorable furry creature that people will want to pet and, in general, think is absolutely precious!

Besides getting to know his new family, your puppy should be exposed to other people, animals and situations, but of course he must not come into close contact with dogs you don't know well until his course of injections is fully complete. This will help him become well adjusted as he grows up and less prone to being timid or fearful of the new things he will encounter. Your pup's socialisation began with the breeder but now it is your responsibility to continue it. The socialisation he receives up until the age of 12 weeks is the most critical, as this is the time when he forms his impressions of the outside world. Be especially careful during the eight-to-ten-week period, also known as the fear period. The interaction he receives during this time should be gentle and reassuring. Lack of socialisation can manifest itself in fear and aggression as the dog grows up. He needs lots of human contact, affection, handling and exposure to other animals.

Once your pup has received his necessary vaccinations, feel free to take him out and about

Your Puppy

(on his lead, of course). Walk him around the neighbourhood, take him on your daily errands, let people pet him, let him meet other dogs and pets, etc. Puppies do not have to try to make friends; there will be no shortage of people who will want to introduce themselves. Just make sure that you carefully supervise each meeting. If the neighbourhood children want to say hello, for example, that is great—children and pups most often make great companions. Sometimes an excited child can unintentionally handle a pup too roughly, or an overzealous pup can playfully nip a little too hard. You want to make socialisation experiences positive ones. What a pup learns during this very formative stage will affect his attitude toward future encounters. You want your dog to be comfortable around everyone. A pup that has a bad experience with a child may grow up to be a dog that is shy around or aggressive toward children.

MANNERS MATTER
During the socialisation process, a puppy should meet people, experience different environments and definitely be exposed to other canines. Through playing and interacting with other dogs, your puppy will learn lessons, ranging from controlling the pressure of his jaws by biting his litter mates to the inner-workings of the canine pack that he will apply to his human relationships for the rest of his life. That is why removing a puppy from its litter too early (before eight weeks) can be detrimental to the pup's development.

STRESS-FREE
Some experts in canine health advise that stress during a dog's early years of development can compromise and weaken his immune system and may trigger the potential for a shortened life expectancy. They emphasise the need for happy and stress-free growing-up years.

CONSISTENCY IN TRAINING
Dogs, being pack animals, naturally need a leader, or else they try to establish dominance in their packs. When you welcome a dog into your family,

BOY OR GIRL?

An important consideration to be discussed is the sex of your puppy. For a family companion, a bitch may be the better choice, considering the female's inbred concern for all young creatures and her accompanying tolerance and patience. It is always advisable to spay a pet bitch, which may guarantee her a longer life.

the choice of who becomes the leader and who becomes the 'pack' is entirely up to you! Your pup's intuitive quest for dominance, coupled with the fact that it is nearly impossible to look at an adorable Shar Pei pup with his 'puppy-dog' eyes and not cave in, give the pup almost an unfair advantage in getting the upper hand! A pup will definitely test the waters to see what he can and cannot do. Do not give in to those pleading eyes—stand your ground when it comes to disciplining the pup and make sure that all family members do the same. It will only confuse the pup when Mother tells him to get off the sofa when he is used to sitting up there with Father to watch the nightly news. Avoid discrepancies by having all members of the household decide on the rules before the pup even comes home…and be consistent in enforcing them! Early training shapes the dog's personality, so you cannot be unclear in what you expect.

COMMON PUPPY PROBLEMS

The best way to prevent puppy problems is to be proactive in stopping an undesirable behaviour as soon as it starts. The old saying 'You can't teach an old dog new tricks' does not necessarily hold true, but it is true that it is much easier to

Your Puppy

> **TRAINING TIP**
> Training your puppy takes much patience and can be frustrating at times, but you should see results from your efforts. If you have a puppy that seems untrainable, take him to a trainer or behaviourist. The dog may have a personality problem that requires the help of a professional, or perhaps you need help in learning how to train your dog.

discourage bad behaviour in a young developing pup than to wait until the pup's bad behaviour becomes the adult dog's bad habit. There are some problems that are especially prevalent in puppies as they develop.

NIPPING

As puppies start to teethe, they feel the need to sink their teeth into anything available… unfortunately that includes your fingers, arms, hair and toes. You may find this behaviour cute for the first five seconds…until you feel just how sharp those puppy teeth are. This is something you want to discourage immediately and consistently with a firm 'No!' (or whatever number of firm 'No's' it takes for him to understand that you mean business). Then replace your finger with an appropriate chew toy. While this behaviour is merely annoying when the dog is young, it can become dangerous as your Shar Pei's adult teeth grow in and his jaws develop, and he continues to think it is okay to gnaw on human appendages. Your Shar Pei does not mean any harm with a friendly nip, but he also does not know his own strength.

CRYING/WHINING

Your pup will often cry, whine, whimper, howl or make some type of commotion when he is left alone. This is basically his way of calling out for attention to make sure that you know he is there and that you have not forgotten about him. He feels insecure when he is left alone, when you are out of the house and he is in his crate or when you are in another part of the house and he cannot see you. The noise he is making is an expression of the anxiety he feels at being alone, so he needs to be taught that being alone is

Socialising the puppy with children and adults is tantamount to having a reliable grown dog that you can trust no matter what the situation.

HOW VACCINES WORK

If you've just bought a puppy, you surely know the importance of having your pup vaccinated, but do you understand how vaccines work? Vaccines contain the same bacteria or viruses that cause the disease you want to prevent, but they have been chemically modified so that they don't cause any harm. Instead, the vaccine causes your dog to produce antibodies that fight the harmful bacteria. Thus, if your pup is exposed to the disease in the future, the antibodies will destroy the viruses or bacteria.

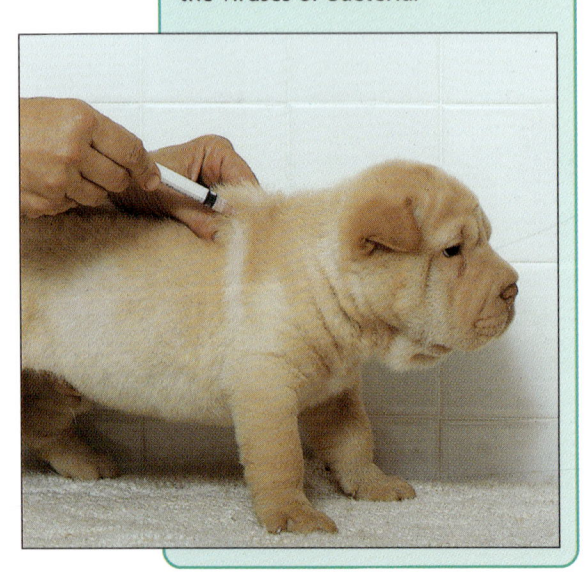

okay. You are not actually training the dog to stop making noise, you are training him to feel comfortable when he is alone and thus removing the need for him to make the noise. This is where the crate with cosy bedding and a toy comes in handy. You want to know that he is safe when you are not there to supervise, and you know that he will be safe in his crate rather than roaming freely

Your Puppy

about the house. In order for the pup to stay in his crate without making a fuss, he needs to be comfortable in his crate. On that note, it is extremely important that the crate is never used as a form of punishment, or the pup will have a negative association with the crate.

Accustom the pup to the crate in short, gradually increasing time intervals in which you put him in the crate, maybe with a treat, and stay in the room with him. If he cries or makes a fuss, do not go to him, but stay in his sight. Gradually he will realise that staying in his crate is all right without your help, and it will not be so traumatic for him when you are not around. You may want to leave the radio on softly when you leave the house; the sound of human voices may be comforting to him.

You have to see it to believe it... a Shar Pei making the acquaintance of a peacock!

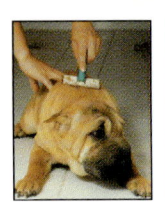

Everyday Care of Your
SHAR PEI

FEEDING

SPECIAL CONSIDERATIONS

It is important not to overfeed your Shar Pei, for it could easily become overweight and this would put a strain both on the heart and on the joints. An overweight Shar Pei may have less resistance to viral infections, and any overweight dog is at greater risk under anaesthesia.

Sometimes a Shar Pei may put on too much weight when fed on proprietary foods, in which case the intake should be cut back and low-calorie foods such as low-fat cottage cheese, green beans and other cooked vegetables can be used as substitutes.

Shar Pei enjoy boiled fish (without bones of course!), tinned fish, chicken, turkey, rabbit and lightly scrambled egg. Rice pudding and cottage cheese also appear to be firm favourites.

A Shar Pei should not be over-dosed with vitamins and additives; this only serves to unbalance an otherwise balanced proprietary diet. However, some Shar Pei owners do like to give their puppies and young dogs one vitamin C tablet each day, taken with food. At the age of about a year this should be replaced with a teaspoonful of cod-liver oil and malt. It is believed that Shar Pei should not be fed flaked maize or maize oil.

Plain brown rice is good if boiled; indeed, many Shar Pei owners find that a chicken and

FEEDING TIP
You must store your dried dog food carefully. Open packages of dog food quickly lose their vitamin value, usually within 90 days of being opened. Mould spores and vermin could also contaminate the food.

Everyday Care

FOOD PREFERENCE

Selecting the best dried dog food is difficult. There is no majority consensus among veterinary scientists as to the value of nutrient analyses (protein, fat, fibre, moisture, ash, cholesterol, minerals, etc.). All agree that feeding trials are what matters, but you also have to consider the individual dog. Its weight, age, activity and what pleases its taste, all must be considered. It is probably best to take the advice of your veterinary surgeon. Every dog's dietary requirements vary, even during the lifetime of a particular dog.

If your dog is fed a good dried food, it does not require supplements of meat or vegetables. Dogs do appreciate a little variety in their diets so you may choose to stay with the same brand, but vary the flavour. Alternatively you may wish to add a little flavoured stock to give a difference to the taste.

Shar Pei that tend to gulp their food should be fed two small portions a day, rather than just one meal. Bloat, or to give it its proper name, gastric torsion, is always a greater risk if dogs gulp their food, so one should always keep an eye on one's dog at mealtimes. Meals should never be fed within an hour of strenuous exercise.

FOOD CHOICES FOR SHAR PEI

Today the choices of food for your Shar Pei are many and varied. There are simply dozens of brands of food in all sorts of flavours and textures, ranging from puppy diets to those for seniors. There are even hypoallergenic and low-calorie diets available. Because your Shar Pei's food has a bearing on coat, health and temperament, it is essential that the most suitable diet is selected for a Shar Pei of his age. It is fair to say,

Puppies can be offered a dried food shortly after they have been weaned. Select a brand that is properly balanced and formulated for puppies.

rice or lamb and rice diet suits them well. Raw vegetables are also highly nutritious, so grated raw vegetables are always a suitable and usually welcome alternative to cooked ones.

Many Shar Pei owners also like to use seaweed powder, also known as kelp, as a supplement. This has many beneficial properties and can be an aid to preserving good pigment.

TEST FOR PROPER DIET

A good test for proper diet is the colour, odour and firmness of your dog's stool. A healthy dog usually produces three semi-hard stools per day. The stools should have no unpleasant odour. They should be the same colour from excretion to excretion.

'DOES THIS COLLAR MAKE ME LOOK FAT?'

While humans may obsess about how they look and how trim their bodies are, many people believe that extra weight on their dogs is a good thing. The truth is, pets should not be over- or under-weight, as both can lead to or signal sickness. In order to tell how fit your pet is, run your hands over his ribs. Are his ribs buried under a layer of fat or are they sticking out considerably? If your pet is within his normal weight range, you should be able to feel the ribs easily. If you stand above him, the outline of his body should resemble an hourglass. Some breeds do tend to be leaner; while some are a bit stockier, but making sure your dog is the right weight for his breed will certainly contribute to his good health.

however, that even experienced owners can be perplexed by the enormous range of foods available. Only understanding what is best for your dog will help you reach a valued decision.

Dog foods are produced in three basic types: dried, semi-moist and tinned. Dried foods are useful for the cost-conscious for overall they tend to be less expensive than semi-moist or tinned. They also contain the least fat and the most preservatives. In general, tinned foods are made up of 60–70 percent water, while semi-moist ones often contain so much sugar that they are perhaps the least preferred by owners, even though their dogs seem to like them.

When selecting your dog's diet, three stages of development must be considered: the puppy stage, adult stage and the senior or veteran stage.

A proper diet will be evident in your Shar Pei's coat. It should look shiny and healthy, never dull or dry.

PUPPY STAGE

Puppies instinctively want to suck milk from their mother's teats and a normal puppy will exhibit this behaviour from just a few moments following birth. If puppies do not attempt to suckle within the first half-hour or so, they should be encouraged to do so by placing them on the nipples, having selected ones with plenty of milk. This early milk supply is important in providing colostrum to protect the puppies during the first eight to ten weeks of their lives. Although a mother's milk is much better than any milk formula, despite there being some excellent ones available, if the puppies do not feed, you will have to feed them yourself. For those with less experience, advice from a veterinary surgeon is important so that you feed not only the right quantity of milk but that of correct quality, fed at suitably frequent intervals, usually every two hours during the first few days of life.

Puppies should be allowed to nurse from their mothers for about the first six weeks, although from the third or fourth week you should begin to introduce small portions of suitable solid food. Most breeders like to introduce alternate milk and meat meals initially, building up to weaning time.

GRAIN-BASED DIETS

Some less expensive dog foods are based on grains and other plant proteins. While these products may appear to be attractively priced, many breeders prefer a diet based on animal proteins and believe that they are more conducive to your dog's health. Many grain-based diets rely on soy protein that may cause flatulence (passing gas).

There are many cases, however, when your dog might require a special diet. These special requirements should only be recommended by your veterinary surgeon.

By the time the puppies are seven or a maximum of eight weeks old, they should be fully weaned and fed solely on a proprietary puppy food. Selection of the most suitable, good-quality diet at this time is essential, for a puppy's fastest growth rate is during the first year of life. Veterinary surgeons are usually able to offer advice in this regard and, although the frequency of meals will have been reduced over time, only when a young dog has reached the age of about 12 months should an adult diet be fed.

Puppy and junior diets should be well balanced for the needs of your dog, so that except in certain circumstances additional vitamins, minerals and proteins will not be required.

ADULT DIETS

A dog is considered an adult when it has stopped growing, so in general the diet of a Shar Pei can be changed to an adult one at about 10 to 12 months of age. Again you should rely upon your veterinary surgeon or dietary specialist to recommend an acceptable maintenance diet. Major dog food manufacturers specialise in this type of food, and it is merely necessary for you to select the one best suited to your dog's needs. Active dogs

Shar Pei are hardy eaters but should not be allowed to gulp their food. Each dog should be fed from his own bowl to avoid competition at meal time.

Everyday Care

may have different requirements than sedate dogs.

Senior Diets

As dogs get older, their metabolism changes. The older dog usually exercises less, moves more slowly and sleeps more. This change in lifestyle and physiological performance requires a change in diet. Since these changes take place slowly, they might not be recognisable. What is easily recognisable is weight gain. By continuing to feed your dog an adult-maintenance diet when it is slowing down metabolically, your dog will gain weight. Obesity in an older dog compounds the health problems that already accompany old age.

As your dog gets older, few of his organs function up to par. The kidneys slow down and the intestines become less efficient. These age-related factors are best handled with a change in diet and a change in feeding schedule to give smaller portions that are more easily digested.

There is no single best diet for every older dog. While many dogs do well on light or senior diets, other dogs do better on puppy diets or other special premium diets such as lamb

> **FEEDING TIP**
> Dog food must be at room temperature, neither too hot nor too cold. Fresh water, changed daily and served in a clean bowl, is mandatory, especially when feeding dried food.
>   Never feed your dog from the table while you are eating. Never feed your dog leftovers from your own meal. They usually contain too much fat and too much seasoning.
>   Dogs must chew their food. Hard pellets are excellent; soups and slurries are to be avoided.
>   Don't add left-overs or any extras to normal dog food. The normal food is usually balanced and adding something extra destroys the balance.
>   Except for age-related changes, dogs do not require dietary variations. They can be fed the same diet, day after day, without their becoming ill.

> **CHANGE IN DIET**
> As your dog's caretaker, you know the importance of keeping his diet consistent, but sometimes when you run out of food or if you're on holiday, you have to make a change quickly. Some dogs will experience digestive problems but most will not. If you are planning on changing your dog's menu, do so gradually to ensure that your dog will not have any problems. Over a period of four to five days, slowly add some new food to your dog's old food, increasing the percentage of new food each day.

and rice. Be sensitive to your senior Shar Pei's diet and this will help control other problems that may arise with your old friend.

WATER

Just as your dog needs proper nutrition from his food, water is an essential 'nutrient' as well. Water keeps the dog's body properly hydrated and promotes normal function of the body's systems. During housebreaking it is necessary to keep an eye on how much water your Shar Pei is drinking, but once he is reliably trained he should have access to clean fresh water at all

> **DO DOGS HAVE TASTE BUDS?**
> Watching a dog 'wolf' or gobble his food, seemingly without chewing, leads an owner to wonder whether their dogs can taste anything. Yes, dogs have taste buds, with sensory perception of sweet, salty and sour. Puppies are born with fully mature taste buds.

> **DRINK, DRANK, DRUNK— MAKE IT A DOUBLE**
> In both humans and dogs, as well as most living organisms, water forms the major part of nearly every body tissue. Naturally, we take water for granted, but without it, life as we know it would cease.
>
> For dogs, water is needed to keep their bodies functioning biochemically. Additionally, water is needed to replace the water lost while panting. Unlike humans who are able to sweat to dissipate heat, dogs must pant to cool down, thereby losing the vital water from their bodies needed to regulate their body temperatures. Humans lose electrolyte-containing products and other body-fluid components through sweating; dogs do not lose anything except water.
>
> Water is essential always, but especially so when the weather is hot or humid or when your dog is exercising or working vigorously.

Everyday Care

times, especially if you feed dried food. Make certain that the dog's water bowl is clean, and change the water often.

EXERCISE
The Shar Pei is a fairly active breed that enjoys exercise, but you don't have to be a marathon runner to keep your Shar Pei in shape. The shoulders of a Shar Pei should be muscular, so when felt they should be firm rather than flabby, though not overloaded. The undercarriage on a Shar Pei should not droop; this is another indication of whether or not your dog is getting the right amount of exercise. Having said that, obviously the undercarriage on a bitch that has recently had a litter will take some time to return to normal.

The Shar Pei enjoys living in the comfort of the house, but apart from regular outings to the garden to do its toilet, a controlled walk on lead each day is also advisable. Ideally it is best to alternate between walking on hard ground and on grass. Regular walks, play sessions in the garden and

The best exercise for any dog is a romp off lead. Only engage in off-lead exercise if the area is completely secured.

TIPPING THE SCALES

Good nutrition is vital to your dog's health, but many people end up over-feeding or giving unnecessary supplements. Here are some common doggie diet don'ts:

- Adding milk, yoghurt and cheese to your dog's diet may seem like a good idea for coat and skin care, but dairy products are very fattening and can cause indigestion.
- Diets high in fat will not cause heart attacks in dogs but will certainly cause your dog to gain weight.
- Most importantly, don't assume your dog will simply stop eating once he doesn't need any more food. Given the chance, he will eat you out of house and home!

letting the dog run free in the garden under your supervision are good forms of exercise for the Shar Pei. For those who are more ambitious, you will find that your Shar Pei also enjoys long walks, an occasional hike, games of fetch or even a swim! Swimming is an activity that is especially enjoyed by Shar Pei and can help to keep them trim, but swimming must always be carefully supervised.

Bear in mind that an overweight dog should never be suddenly over-exercised; instead he should be encouraged to increase exercise slowly. Not only is exercise essential to keep the dog's body fit, it is essential to his mental well being. A bored dog will find something to do, which often manifests itself in some type of destructive behaviour. In this sense, exercise is essential for the owner's mental well-being as well!

Shar Pei can also create their own exercise, either by playing with a suitable safe toy, or by playing with other dogs. Always remember that the Shar Pei is an intelligent breed and, apart from the physical benefit, exercise is also needed to stimulate the mind.

GROOMING

The coarseness of a Shar Pei's coat tends to repel dirt and

What are you feeding your dog?

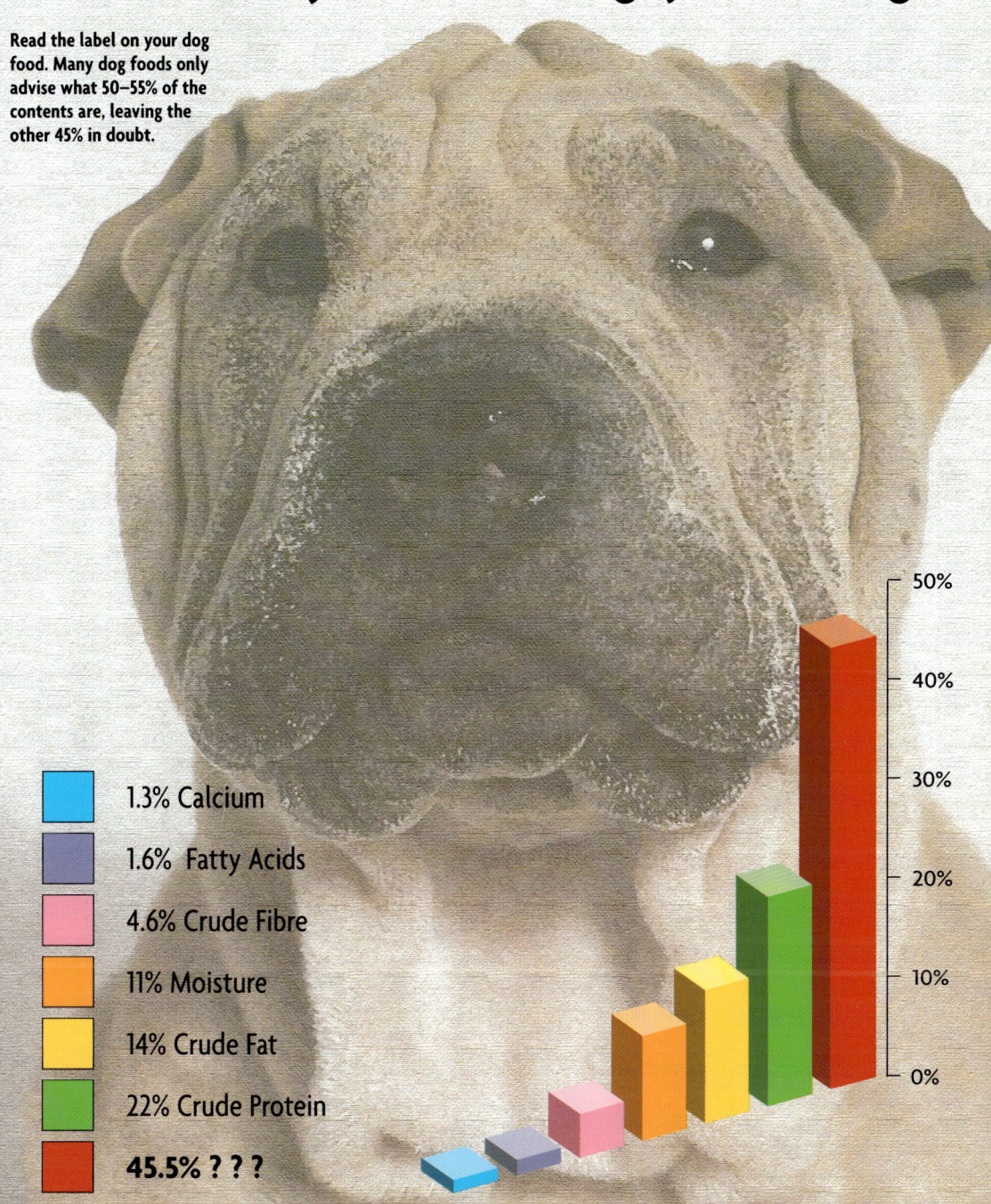

Read the label on your dog food. Many dog foods only advise what 50–55% of the contents are, leaving the other 45% in doubt.

- 1.3% Calcium
- 1.6% Fatty Acids
- 4.6% Crude Fibre
- 11% Moisture
- 14% Crude Fat
- 22% Crude Protein
- 45.5% ? ? ?

Your local pet shop will carry various types of brushes, which will make the grooming job a pleasure for both you and your dog.

fortunately it is a coat that doesn't seem to give off a doggy odour. The shortness of the coat means also that it does not mat, so it is not necessary to brush the coat to excess. To keep the coat healthy and in good condition, it should be brushed lightly with either a pure bristle brush or a grooming mitten.

Although light-coloured dogs can look fresher if they have had a bath before a show, it is not really necessary to bath a Shar Pei frequently. Indeed, some owners like to bath their dogs about every two weeks, but the majority of Shar Pei are bathed perhaps two, three or four times a year. Important times for bathing are before, or before and after, each moult.

GROOMING EQUIPMENT

How much grooming equipment you purchase will depend on how much grooming you are going to do. Here are some basics:
- Natural bristle brush
- Slicker brush
- Metal comb
- Scissors
- Blaster
- Rubber mat
- Dog shampoo
- Spray hose attachment
- Ear cleaner
- Cotton wipes
- Towels
- Nail clippers

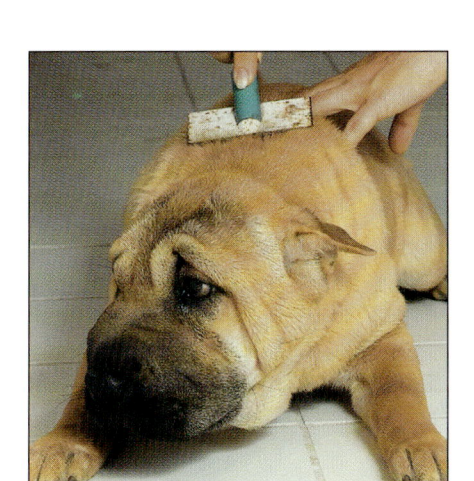

Everyday Care

A rake is effective for removing loose hairs and dirt from your Shar Pei's coat.

Occasional bathing assists in retaining oils in the coat while eliminating dead or loose hair. A good idea for freshening up a dark coloured dog is to wipe the coat over with a wet towel. Bathing too frequently will remove too much natural oil from the coat.

Some Shar Pei are reputed to have something of an aversion to water, so it is perhaps wise to give a puppy its first bath while it is still fairly young. This way it will become accustomed to bathing by the time it reaches maturity.

BATHING

Dogs do not need to be bathed as often as humans, but occasional bathing is essential for healthy skin and a healthy, shiny coat. Again, like most anything, if you accustom your pup to being bathed as a puppy, it will be second nature by the time he grows up. You want your dog to be at ease in the bath or else it could end up a wet, soapy, messy ordeal for both of you!

Brush your Shar Pei thoroughly before wetting his coat. This will get rid of most mats and tangles, which are harder to remove when the coat is wet. Make certain that your dog has a good non-slip surface to stand on. Begin by wetting the dog's coat. A shower or hose attachment is necessary for thoroughly wetting and rinsing the coat. Check the water temperature to make sure that it is neither too hot nor too cold.

Next, apply shampoo to the dog's coat and work it into a good lather. You should purchase a shampoo that is

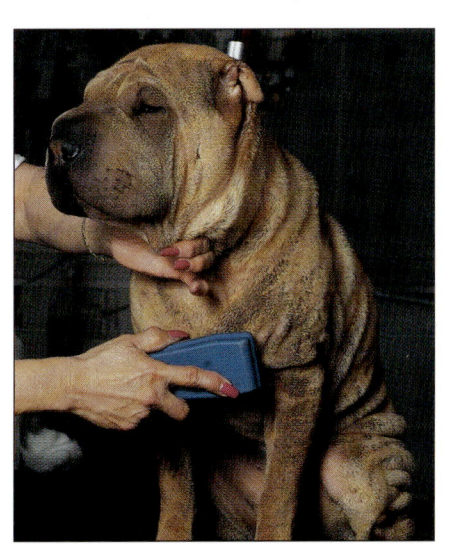

If your Shar Pei is accustomed to being brushed while he is a puppy, he will patiently endure his grooming session as an adult.

BATHING BEAUTY

Once you are sure that the dog is thoroughly rinsed, squeeze the excess water out of the coat with your hand and dry him with a heavy towel. You may choose to use a blaster on his coat or just let it dry naturally. In cold weather, never allow your dog outside with a wet coat.

There are 'dry bath' products on the market, which are sprays and powders intended for spot cleaning, that can be used between regular baths, if necessary. They are not substitutes for regular baths, but they are easy to use for touch-ups as they do not require rinsing.

made for dogs. Do not use a product made for human hair. Wash the head last; you do not want shampoo to drip into the dog's eyes while you are washing the rest of his body. Work the shampoo all the way down to the skin. You can use this opportunity to check the skin for any bumps, bites or other abnormalities. Do not neglect any area of the body—get all of the hard-to-reach places.

Once the dog has been thoroughly shampooed, he requires an equally thorough rinsing. Shampoo left in the coat can be irritating to the skin. Protect his eyes from the shampoo by shielding them with your hand and directing the flow of water in the opposite direction. You should also avoid getting water in the ear canal. Be prepared for your dog to shake out his coat—you might want to stand back, but make sure you have a hold on the dog to keep him from running through the house.

Wipe the eyes gently with cotton wool.

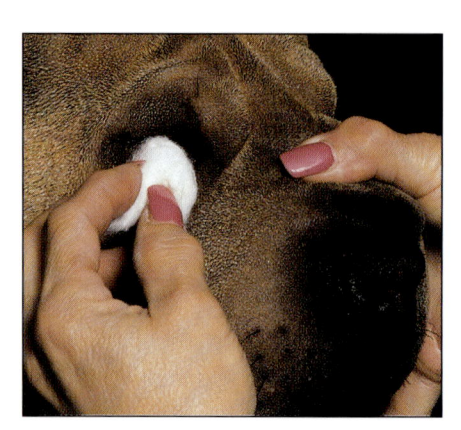

SOAP IT UP

The use of human soap products like shampoo, bubble bath and hand soap can be damaging to a dog's coat and skin. Human products are too strong and remove the protective oils coating the dog's hair and skin (making him water-resistant). Use only shampoo made especially for dogs and you may like to use a medicated shampoo, which will always help to keep external parasites at bay.

Everyday Care

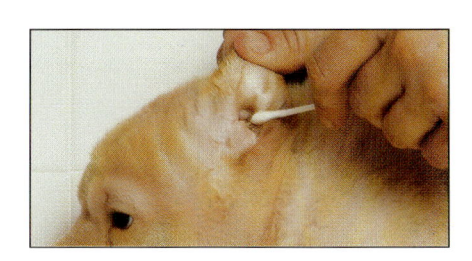

EARS
Ears must be checked on a weekly basis because, being small, they can be prone to picking up infection. Good proprietary ear cleaning products are now available. These should be applied with cotton wool, taking care not to probe too deeply into the ear for fear of injury.

EYES
Eyes, too, must be kept scrupulously clean, making sure to use a different piece of cotton wool for each eye, so that any possible infection is not transferred.

TEETH
A Shar Pei enjoys chewing on hard biscuits or suitable safe chews. This helps greatly in keeping teeth clean and free from tartar. Provided you have been carefully trained by someone who knows how to use a tooth scraper, you may like to use this yourself as an efficient way of removing tartar. Otherwise, or possibly in addition, your Shar Pei's teeth should be brushed regularly using a canine toothpaste.

NAILS
Nails will need a weekly check. Provided that you have practised cutting your dog's nails since puppyhood, this should not present any problem, so long as you take care not to accidentally cut the quick. If you do accidentally cause a nail to bleed, you can apply potassium permanganate, always useful to keep in your veterinary medicine cabinet in case of emergency. Should you not have any, apparently household flour will also help to stem bleeding.

There are two types of nail clippers, straight edged and 'guillotine.' Personally I have always found the latter obtain a better finish and are easier to use. If your Shar Pei is regularly exercised on a hard surface, you may well find that the nails wear down naturally, but still they must be checked from time to time.

Clean the ears regularly. A piece of soft cotton wool is preferable to a cotton bud; it poses less of a risk of probing into the ear.

Start clipping the dog's nails when it is still a puppy in order to acclimate it to the process. Some dogs do not like having their feed touched, so it's best to desensitise them to it early on.

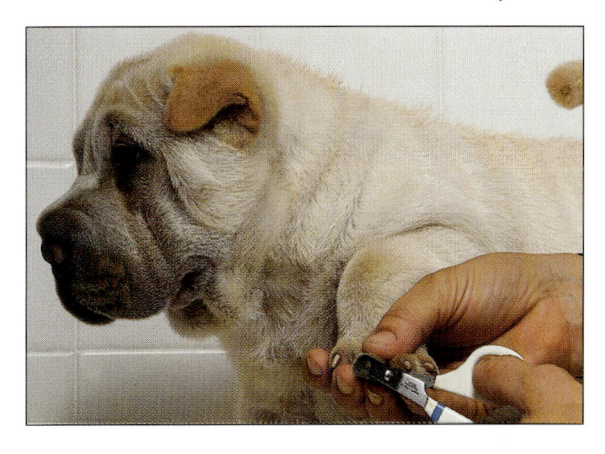

Nail Maintenance

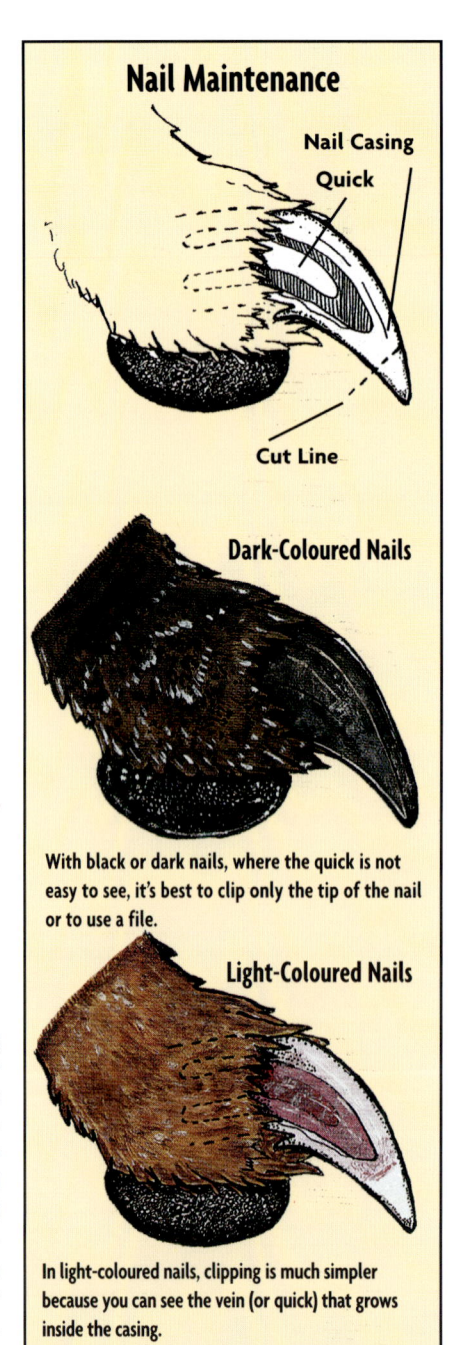

- Nail Casing
- Quick
- Cut Line

Dark-Coloured Nails

With black or dark nails, where the quick is not easy to see, it's best to clip only the tip of the nail or to use a file.

Light-Coloured Nails

In light-coloured nails, clipping is much simpler because you can see the vein (or quick) that grows inside the casing.

Bring along some of your Shar Pei's toys when travelling. Familiar objects will make him feel more comfortable in an unfamiliar place.

PEDICURE TIP

A dog that spends a lot of time outside on a hard surface, such as cement or pavement, will have his nails naturally worn down and may not need to have them trimmed as often, except maybe in the colder months when he is not outside as much. Regardless, it is best to get your dog accustomed to this procedure at an early age so that he is used to it. Some dogs are especially sensitive about having their feet touched, but if a dog has experienced it since he was young, he should not be bothered by it.

TRAVELLING WITH YOUR DOG

CAR TRAVEL

You should accustom your Shar Pei to riding in a car at an early age. You may or may not take him in the car often, but at the very least he will need to go to the vet and you do not want these trips to be traumatic for the dog or troublesome for you. The safest way for a dog to ride

ON THE ROAD

If you are going on a long motor trip with your dog, be sure the hotels are dog friendly. Many hotels do not accept dogs. Also take along some ice that can be thawed and offered to your dog if he becomes overheated. Most dogs like to lick ice.

the vehicle—this is very dangerous! If you should stop short, your dog can be thrown and injured. If the dog starts climbing on you and pestering you while you are driving, you will not be able to concentrate on the road. It is an unsafe situation for everyone—human and canine.

For long trips, be prepared to stop to let the dog relieve in the car is in his crate. If he uses a crate in the house, you can use the same crate for travel.

Put the pup in the crate and see how he reacts. If he seems uneasy, you can have a passenger hold him on his lap while you drive. Another option is a specially made safety harness for dogs, which straps the dog in much like a seat belt. Do not let the dog roam loose in

TRAVEL TIP

The most extensive travel you do with your dog may be limited to trips to the veterinary surgeon's office—or you may decide to bring him along for long distances when the family goes on holiday. Whichever the case, it is important to consider your dog's safety while travelling.

> **EXERCISE ALERT!**
> You should be careful where you exercise your dog. Many countryside areas have been sprayed with chemicals that are highly toxic to both dogs and humans. Never allow your dog to eat grass or drink from puddles on either public or private grounds, as the run-off water may contain chemicals from sprays and herbicides.

himself. Take with you whatever you need to clean up after him, including some paper kitchen towels and perhaps some old towelling for use should he have an accident in the car or suffer from travel sickness.

AIR TRAVEL

While it is possible to take a dog on a flight within Britain, this is fairly unusual and advance permission is always required. The dog will be required to travel in a fibreglass crate and you should always check in advance with the airline regarding specific requirements. To help the dog be at ease, put one of his favourite toys in the crate with him. Do not feed the dog for at least six hours before the trip to minimise his need to relieve himself. However, certain regulations specify that water must always be made available to the dog in the crate.

Make sure your dog is properly identified and that your contact information appears on his ID tags and on his crate. Animals travel in a different area of the plane than human passengers so every rule must be strictly adhered to so as to prevent the risk of getting separated from your dog.

BOARDING

So you want to take a family holiday—and you want to

> **TRAVEL TIP**
> When travelling, never let your dog off-lead in a strange area. Your dog could run away out of fear or decide to chase a passing squirrel or cat or simply want to stretch his legs without restriction—you might never see your canine friend again.

Everyday Care

VACCINATIONS
For international travel you will have to make arrangements well in advance (perhaps months), as countries' regulations pertaining to bringing in animals differ. There may be special health certificates and/or vaccinations that your dog will need before taking the trip; sometimes this has to be done within a certain time frame. In rabies-free countries, you will need to bring proof of the dog's rabies vaccination and there may be a quarantine period upon arrival.

include *all* members of the family. You would probably make arrangements for accommodation ahead of time anyway, but this is especially important when travelling with a dog. You do not want to make an overnight stop at the only place around for miles and find out that they do not allow dogs. Also, you do not want to reserve a place for your family without confirming that you are travelling with a dog because if it is against their policy you may not have a place to stay.

Select a boarding kennel that meets your standard of excellence. Do not compromise when it comes to leaving your beloved Shar Pei in someone else's care.

IDENTIFICATION

If your dog gets lost, he is not able to ask for directions home.

Identification tags fastened to the collar give important information—the dog's name, the owner's name, the owner's address and a telephone number where the owner can be reached. This makes it easy for whomever finds the dog to contact the owner and arrange to have the dog returned. An added advantage is that a person will be more likely to approach a lost dog who has ID tags on his collar; it tells the person that this is somebody's pet rather than a stray. This is the easiest and fastest method of identification provided that the tags stay on the collar and the collar stays on the dog.

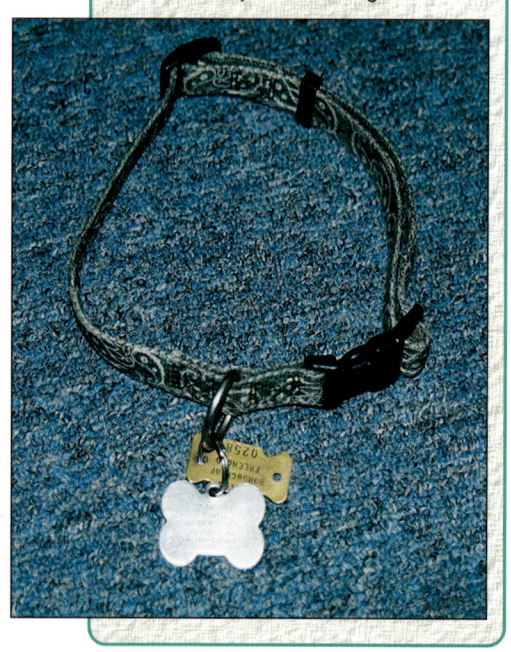

DID YOU KNOW?

You have a valuable dog. If the dog is lost or stolen, you would undoubtedly become extremely upset. If you encounter a lost dog, notify the police or the local animal shelter.

Alternatively, if you are travelling and choose not to bring your Shar Pei, you will have to make arrangements for him while you are away. Some options are to take him to a neighbour's house to stay while you are gone, to have a trusted neighbour pop in often or stay at your house, or bring your dog to a reputable boarding kennel. If you choose to board him at a kennel, you should visit in advance to see the facilities provided, how clean they are and where the dogs are kept. Talk to some of the employees and see how they treat the dogs—do they spend time with the dogs, play with them, exercise them, etc.? Also find out the kennel's policy on vaccinations and what they require. This is for all of the dogs' safety, since when dogs are kept together, there is a greater risk of diseases being passed from dog to dog.

IDENTIFICATION

Your Shar Pei is your valued companion and friend. That is

Everyday Care

why you always keep a close eye on him and you have made sure that he cannot escape from the garden or wriggle out of his collar and run away from you. However, accidents can happen and there may come a time when your dog unexpectedly gets separated from you. If this unfortunate event should occur, the first thing on your mind will be finding him. Proper identification, including an ID tag, a tattoo and possibly a microchip, will increase the chances of his being returned to you safely and quickly.

Be certain that your Shar Pei's ID tag is securely fastened to his collar.

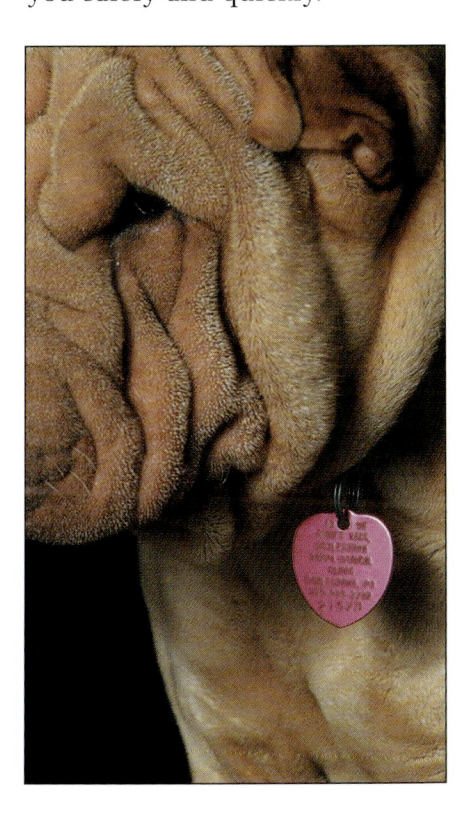

IDENTIFICATION OPTIONS

As puppies become more and more expensive, especially those puppies of high quality for showing and/or breeding, they have a greater chance of being stolen. The usual collar dog tag is, of course, easily removed. But there are two techniques that have become widely used for identification.

The puppy microchip implantation involves the injection of a small microchip, about the size of a corn kernel, under the skin of the dog. If your dog shows up at a clinic or shelter, or is offered for resale under less than savoury circumstances, it can be positively identified by the microchip. The microchip is scanned and a registry quickly identifies you as the owner. This is not only protection against theft, but should the dog run away or go chasing a squirrel and get lost, you have a fair chance of getting it back.

Tattooing is done on various parts of the dog, from its belly to its cheeks. The number tattooed can be your telephone number or any other number which you can easily memorise. When professional dog thieves see a tattooed dog, they usually lose interest in it. Both microchipping and tattooing can be done at your local veterinary clinic. For the safety of our dogs, no laboratory facility or dog broker will accept a tattooed dog as stock.

Housebreaking and Training Your
SHAR PEI

Living with an untrained dog is a lot like owning a piano that you do not know how to play—it is a nice object to look at but it does not do much more than that to bring you pleasure. Now try taking piano lessons and suddenly the piano comes alive and brings forth magical sounds and rhythms that set your heart singing and your body swaying.

The same is true with your Shar Pei. Any dog is a big responsibility and if not trained sensibly may develop unacceptable behaviour that annoys you or could even cause family friction.

To train your Shar Pei, you may like to enrol in an obedience class. Teach him good manners as you learn how and why he behaves the way he does. Find out how to communicate with your dog and how to recognise and understand his communications with you. Suddenly the dog takes on a new role in your life—he is clever, interesting, well behaved and fun to be with. He demonstrates his bond of devotion to you daily. In other words, your Shar Pei does wonders for your ego because

> **FAMILY TIES**
> If you have other pets in the home and/or interact often with the pets of friends and other family members, your pup will respond to those pets in much the same manner as you do. It is only when you show fear of or resentment toward another animal that he will act fearful or unfriendly.

he constantly reminds you that you are not only his leader, you are his hero!

Those involved with teaching dog obedience and counselling owners about their dogs' behaviour have discovered some interesting facts about dog ownership. For example, training dogs when they are puppies results in the highest rate of success in developing well-mannered and well-adjusted adult dogs. Training an older dog, from six months to six years of age, can produce almost equal results providing that the owner accepts the dog's slower rate of learning capability and is willing to work patiently to help the dog succeed at developing to his fullest

Housebreaking and Training

89

Training must begin the instant your Shar Pei enters your home. While owning a dog should be a pleasure first, proper obedience training provides an owner with the best possible companion.

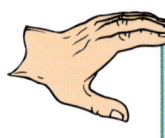

> **THE HAND THAT FEEDS**
> To a dog's way of thinking, your hands are like his mouth in terms of a defence mechanism. If you squeeze him too tightly, he might just bite you because that would be his normal response. This is not aggressive biting and, although all biting should be discouraged, you need the discipline in learning how to handle your dog.

Keeping the dog's attention is the first step in any type of training. A treat will surely make your Shar Pei take notice!

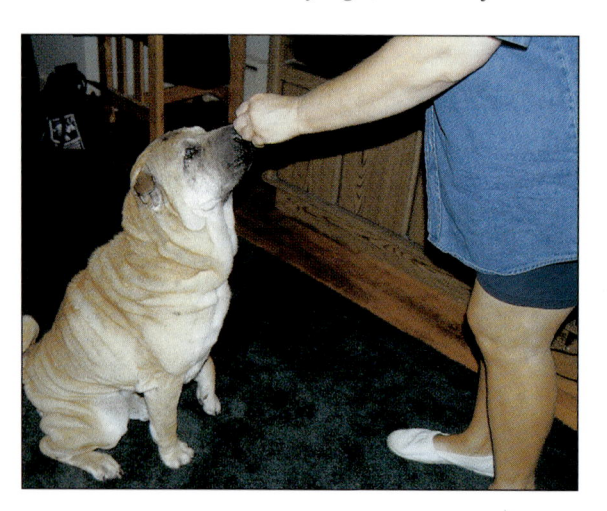

potential. Unfortunately, many owners of untrained adult dogs lack the patience factor, so they do not persist until their dogs are successful at learning particular behaviours.

Training a puppy aged 10 to 16 weeks (20 weeks at the most) is like working with a dry sponge in a pool of water. The pup soaks up whatever you show him and constantly looks for more things to do and learn. At this early age, his body is not yet producing hormones, and therein lies the reason for such a high rate of success. Without hormones, he is focused on his owners and not particularly interested in investigating other places, dogs, people, etc. You are his leader: his provider of food, water, shelter and security. He latches onto you and wants to stay close. He will usually follow you from room to room, will not let you out of his sight when you are outdoors with him and will respond in like manner to the people and animals you encounter. If you greet a friend warmly, he will be happy to greet the person as well. If, however, you are hesitant, even anxious, about the approach of a stranger, he will respond accordingly.

Once the puppy begins to produce hormones, his natural curiosity emerges and he begins to investigate the world around him. It is at this time when you may notice that the untrained

> **HONOUR AND OBEY**
> Dogs are the most honourable animals in existence. They consider another species (humans) as their own. They interface with you. You are their leader. Puppies perceive children to be on their level; their actions around small children are different from their behaviour around their adult masters.

Housebreaking and Training

dog begins to wander away from you and even ignore your commands to stay close. When this behaviour becomes a problem, the owner has two choices: get rid of the dog or train him. It is strongly urged that you choose the latter option.

There are usually classes within a reasonable distance from the owner's home, but you can also do a lot to train your dog yourself. Sometimes there are classes available but the tuition is too costly. Whatever the circumstances, the solution to the problem of lack of lesson availability lies within the pages of this book.

This chapter is devoted to helping you train your Shar Pei at home. If the recommended procedures are followed faithfully, you may expect positive results that will prove rewarding both to you and your dog.

Whether your new charge is a puppy or a mature adult, the methods of teaching and the techniques we use in training basic behaviours are the same. After all, no dog, whether puppy or adult, likes harsh or inhumane methods. All creatures, however, respond favourably to gentle motivational methods and sincere praise and encouragement. Now let us get started.

REAP THE REWARDS

If you start with a normal, healthy dog and give him time, patience and some carefully executed lessons, you will reap the rewards of that training for the life of the dog. And what a life it will be! The two of you will find immeasurable pleasure in the companionship you have built together with love, respect and understanding.

PARENTAL GUIDANCE
Training a dog is a life experience. Many parents admit that much of what they know about raising children they learned from caring for their dogs. Dogs respond to love, fairness and guidance, just as children do. Become a good dog owner and you may become an even better parent.

HOUSEBREAKING
You can train a puppy to relieve itself wherever you choose, but this must be somewhere suitable. You should bear in mind from the outset that when your puppy is old enough to go out in public places, any canine deposits must be removed at once. You will always have to carry with you a small plastic bag or 'poop-scoop.'

Outdoor training includes such surfaces as grass, soil and cement. Indoor training usually means training your dog to newspaper.

When deciding on the surface and location that you will want your Shar Pei to use, be sure it is going to be permanent. Training your dog to grass and then changing your mind two months later is extremely difficult for both dog and owner.

Next, choose the command you will use each and every time you want your puppy to void. 'Hurry up' and 'Toilet' are examples of commands commonly used by dog owners.

Get in the habit of giving the puppy your chosen relief command before you take him out. That way, when he becomes an adult, you will be

DEVELOP A WELL-MANNERED DOG
Dogs will do anything for your attention. If you reward the dog when he is calm and resting, you will develop a well-mannered dog. If, on the other hand, you greet your dog excitedly and encourage him to wrestle with you, the dog will greet you the same way and you will have a hyperactive dog on your hands.

Housebreaking and Training   93

MEALTIME
Mealtime should be a peaceful time for your puppy. Do not put his food and water bowls in a high-traffic area in the house. For example, give him his own little corner of the kitchen where he can eat undisturbed and where he will not be underfoot. Do not allow small children or other family members to disturb the pup when he is eating.

PUPPY'S NEEDS
Puppy needs to relieve himself after play periods, after each meal, after he has been sleeping and at any time he indicates that he is looking for a place to urinate or defecate.

The urinary and intestinal tract muscles of very young puppies are not fully developed. Therefore, like

THINK BEFORE YOU BARK
Dogs are sensitive to their master's moods and emotions. Use your voice wisely when communicating with your dog. Never raise your voice at your dog unless you are angry and trying to correct him. 'Barking' at your dog can become as meaningless as 'dogspeak' is to you. Think before you bark!

able to determine if he wants to go out when you ask him. A confirmation will be signs of interest, wagging his tail, watching you intently, going to the door, etc.

> **PAPER CAPER**
> Never line your pup's sleeping area with newspaper. Puppy litters are usually raised on newspaper and, once in your home, the puppy will immediately associate newspaper with voiding. Never put newspaper on any floor while housetraining, as this will only confuse the puppy. If you are paper-training him, use paper in his designated relief area ONLY. Finally, restrict water intake after evening meals. Offer a few licks at a time—never let a young puppy gulp water after meals.

human babies, puppies need to relieve themselves frequently.

Take your puppy out often—every hour for an eight-week-old, for example, and always immediately after sleeping and eating. The older the puppy, the less often he will need to relieve himself. Finally, as a mature healthy adult, he will require only three to five relief trips per day.

Housing

Since the types of housing and control you provide for your puppy have a direct relationship on the success of housetraining, we consider the various aspects of both before we begin training.

Taking a new puppy home and turning him loose in your house can be compared to turning a child loose in a sports arena and telling the child that the place is all his! The sheer enormity of the place would be too much for him to handle.

Instead, offer the puppy clearly defined areas where he can play, sleep, eat and live. A room of the house where the

> **PRACTICE MAKES PERFECT!**
> - Have training lessons with your dog every day in several short segments—three to five times a day for a few minutes at a time is ideal.
> - Do not have long practice sessions. The dog will become easily bored.
> - Never practise when you are tired, ill, worried or in an otherwise negative mood. This will transmit to the dog and may have an adverse effect on its performance.
>
> Think fun, short and above all POSITIVE! End each session on a high note, rather than a failed exercise, and make sure to give a lot of praise. Enjoy the training and help your dog enjoy it, too.

CANINE DEVELOPMENT SCHEDULE

It is important to understand how and at what age a puppy develops into adulthood. If you are a puppy owner, consult the following Canine Development Schedule to determine the stage of development your puppy is currently experiencing. This knowledge will help you as you work with the puppy in the weeks and months ahead.

Period	Age	Characteristics
First to Third	**Birth to Seven Weeks**	Puppy needs food, sleep and warmth, and responds to simple and gentle touching. Needs mother for security and disciplining. Needs littermates for learning and interacting with other dogs. Pup learns to function within a pack and learns pack order of dominance. Begin socialising with adults and children for short periods. Begins to become aware of its environment.
Fourth	**Eight to Twelve Weeks**	Brain is fully developed. Needs socialising with outside world. Remove from mother and littermates. Needs to change from canine pack to human pack. Human dominance necessary. Fear period occurs between 8 and 16 weeks. Avoid fright and pain.
Fifth	**Thirteen to Sixteen Weeks**	Training and formal obedience should begin. Less association with other dogs, more with people, places, situations. Period will pass easily if you remember this is pup's change-to-adolescence time. Be firm and fair. Flight instinct prominent. Permissiveness and over-disciplining can do permanent damage. Praise for good behaviour.
Juvenile	**Four to Eight Months**	Another fear period about 7 to 8 months of age. It passes quickly, but be cautious of fright and pain. Sexual maturity reached. Dominant traits established. Dog should understand sit, down, come and stay by now.

NOTE: THESE ARE APPROXIMATE TIME FRAMES. ALLOW FOR INDIVIDUAL DIFFERENCES IN PUPPIES.

Crate training provides the dog with structure. A dog that comprehends structure and obedience is the easiest to train.

TAKE THE LEAD
Do not carry your dog to his toilet area. Lead him there on a leash or, better yet, encourage him to follow you to the spot. If you start carrying him to his spot, you might end up doing this routine forever and your dog will have the satisfaction of having trained YOU.

family gathers is the most obvious choice. Puppies are social animals and need to feel a part of the pack right from the start. Hearing your voice, watching you while you are doing things and smelling you nearby are all positive

Crate training has many benefits. Aisde from its use in the home, the crate is a safe haven for your Shar Pei while travelling.

reinforcers that he is now a member of your pack. Usually a family room, the kitchen or a nearby adjoining breakfast area is ideal for providing safety and security for both puppy and owner.

Within that room there should be a smaller area that the puppy can call his own. An alcove, a wire or fibreglass dog crate or a fenced (not boarded!) corner from which he can view the activities of his new family will be fine. The size of the area

Housebreaking and Training

or crate is the key factor here. The area must be large enough for the puppy to lie down and stretch out as well as stand up without rubbing his head on the top, yet small enough so that he cannot relieve himself at one end and sleep at the other without coming into contact with his droppings until fully trained to relieve himself outside.

Dogs are, by nature, clean animals and will not remain close to their relief areas unless forced to do so. In those cases, they then become dirty dogs and usually remain that way for life.

The designated area should contain clean bedding and a toy. Water must always be available, in a non-spill container.

Control

By control, we mean helping the puppy to create a lifestyle pattern that will be compatible to that of his human pack (YOU!). Just as we guide little children to learn our way of life, we must show the puppy when it is time to play, eat, sleep, exercise and even entertain himself.

Your puppy should always sleep in his crate. He should also learn that, during times of household confusion and excessive human activity such as at breakfast when family

COMMAND STANCE
Stand up straight and authoritatively when giving your dog commands. Do not issue commands when lying on the floor or lying on your back on the sofa. If you are on your hands and knees when you give a command, your dog will think you are positioning yourself to play.

members are preparing for the day, he can play by himself in relative safety and comfort in his designated area. Each time you leave the puppy alone, he should understand exactly where he is to stay. Puppies are chewers. They cannot tell the difference between lamp cords, television wires, shoes, table legs, etc. Chewing into a television wire, for example, can be fatal to the puppy while a shorted wire can start a fire in the house.

If the puppy chews on the arm of the chair when he is alone, you will probably discipline him angrily when you get home. Thus, he makes the association that your coming home means he is going to be punished. (He will not remember chewing the chair and is incapable of making the association of the discipline with his naughty deed.)

Other times of excitement,

HOW MANY TIMES A DAY?

AGE	RELIEF TRIPS
To 14 weeks	10
14–22 weeks	8
22–32 weeks	6
Adulthood (dog stops growing)	4

These are estimates, of course, but they are a guide to the MINIMUM opportunities a dog should have each day to relieve itself.

TRAINING RULES

If you want to be successful in training your dog, you have four rules to obey yourself:
1. Develop an understanding of how a dog thinks.
2. Do not blame the dog for lack of communication.
3. Define your dog's personality and act accordingly.
4. Have patience and be consistent.

such as family parties, etc., can be fun for the puppy providing he can view the activities from the security of his designated area. He is not underfoot and he is not being fed all sorts of titbits that will probably cause him stomach distress, yet he still feels a part of the fun.

Housebreaking and Training

THE SUCCESS METHOD

Success that comes by luck is usually short lived. Success that comes by well-thought-out proven methods is often more easily achieved and permanent. This is the Success Method. It is designed to give you, the puppy owner, a simple yet proven way to help your puppy develop clean living habits and a feeling of security in his new environment.

SCHEDULE

A puppy should be taken to his relief area each time he is released from his designated area, after meals, after a play session and when he first awakens in the morning (at age eight weeks, this can mean 5 a.m.!). The puppy will indicate that he's ready 'to go' by circling or sniffing busily—do not misinterpret these signs. For a puppy less than ten weeks of age, a routine of taking him out every hour is

THE SUCCESS METHOD

1 Tell the puppy 'Crate time!' and place him in the crate with a small treat (a piece of cheese or half of a biscuit). Let him stay in the crate for five minutes while you are in the same room. Then release him and praise lavishly. Never release him when he is fussing. Wait until he is quiet before you let him out.

2 Repeat Step 1 several times a day.

3 The next day, place the puppy in the crate as before. Let him stay there for ten minutes. Do this several times.

4 Continue building time in five-minute increments until the puppy stays in his crate for 30 minutes with you in the room. Always take him to his relief area after prolonged periods in his crate.

5 Now go back to Step 1 and let the puppy stay in his crate for five minutes, this time while you are out of the room.

6 Once again, build crate time in five-minute increments with you out of the room. When the puppy will stay willingly in his crate (he may even fall asleep!) for 30 minutes with you out of the room, he will be ready to stay in it for several hours at a time.

6 Steps to Successful Crate Training

necessary. As the puppy grows, he will be able to wait for longer periods of time.

Keep trips to his relief area short. Stay no more than five or six minutes and then return to the house. If he goes during that time, praise him lavishly and take him indoors immediately. If he does not, but he has an accident when you go back indoors, pick him up immediately, say 'No! No!' and return to his relief area. Wait a few minutes, then return to the house again. Never hit a puppy or rub his face in urine or excrement when he has had an accident!

Once indoors, put the puppy in his crate until you have had time to clean up his accident. Then release him to the family area and watch him more closely than before. Chances are, his accident was a result of your not picking up his signal or waiting too long before offering him the opportunity to relieve himself. Never hold a grudge against the puppy for accidents.

Let the puppy learn that going outdoors means it is time to relieve himself, not play. Once trained, he will be able to play indoors and out and still differentiate between the times for play versus the times for relief.

Help him develop regular hours for naps, being alone, playing by himself and just resting, all in his crate. Encourage him to entertain himself while you are busy with your activities. Let him learn that having you near is comforting, but it is not your main purpose in life to provide

> **THE CLEAN LIFE**
> By providing sleeping and resting quarters that fit the dog, and offering frequent opportunities to relieve himself outside his quarters, the puppy quickly learns that the outdoors (or the newspaper if you are training him to paper) is the place to go when he needs to urinate or defecate. It also reinforces his innate desire to keep his sleeping quarters clean. This, in turn, helps develop the muscle control that will eventually produce a dog with clean living habits.

Your Shar Pei will return to the same location in the garden to do his business.

Housebreaking and Training

him with undivided attention.

Each time you put a puppy in his own area, use the same command, whatever suits best. Soon he will run to his crate or special area when he hears you say those words.

Crate training provides safety for you, the puppy and the home. It also provides the puppy with a feeling of security, and that helps the puppy achieve self-confidence and clean habits.

Remember that one of the primary ingredients in housetraining your puppy is control. Regardless of your lifestyle, there will always be occasions when you will need to have a place where your dog can stay and be happy and safe. Crate training is the answer for now and in the future.

> **HOUSEBREAKING TIP**
> Most of all, be consistent. Always take your dog to the same location, always use the same command, and always have him on lead when he is in his relief area, unless a fenced-in garden is available.
> By following the Success Method, your puppy will be completely housetrained by the time his muscle and brain development reach maturity. Keep in mind that small breeds usually mature faster than large breeds, but all puppies should be trained by six months of age.

In conclusion, a few key elements are really all you need for a successful house training method—consistency, frequency, praise, control and supervision. By following these procedures with a normal, healthy puppy, you and the puppy will soon be past the stage of 'accidents' and ready to move on to a full and rewarding life together.

Always take time out for fun! Remember, that's why you got a dog in the first place.

ROLES OF DISCIPLINE, REWARD AND PUNISHMENT

Discipline, training one to act in accordance with rules, brings order to life. It is as simple as that. Without discipline, particularly in a group society, chaos reigns supreme and the group will eventually perish. Humans

Always clean up after your dog, whether you're in a public place or your own garden.

> **ATTENTION!**
> Your dog is actually training you at the same time you are training him. Dogs do things to get attention. They usually repeat whatever succeeds in getting your attention.

and canines are social animals and need some form of discipline in order to function effectively. They must procure food, protect their home base and their young and reproduce to keep the species going.

If there were no discipline in the lives of social animals, they would eventually die from starvation and/or predation by other stronger animals.

In the case of domestic canines, dogs need discipline in their lives in order to understand how their pack (you and other family members) functions and how they must act in order to survive.

A large humane society in a highly populated area recently surveyed dog owners regarding their satisfaction with their relationships with their dogs. People who had trained their dogs were 75% more satisfied with their pets than those who had never trained their dogs.

Dr Edward Thorndike, a psychologist, established *Thorndike's Theory of Learning*, which states that a behaviour that results in a pleasant event tends to be repeated. A behaviour that results in an unpleasant event tends not to be repeated. It is this theory on which training methods are based today. For example, if you manipulate a dog to perform a specific behaviour and reward him for doing it, he is likely to do it again because he enjoyed the end result.

Occasionally, punishment, a penalty inflicted for an offence, is necessary. The best type of punishment often comes from an outside source. For example, a child is told not to touch the stove because he may get burned. He disobeys and touches the stove. In doing so,

> **OPEN MINDS**
> Dogs are as different from each other as people are. What works for one dog may not work for another. Have an open mind. If one method of training is unsuccessful, try another.

he receives a burn. From that time on, he respects the heat of the stove and avoids contact with it. Therefore, a behaviour that results in an unpleasant event tends not to be repeated.

A good example of a dog learning the hard way is the dog who chases the house cat. He is told many times to leave the cat alone, yet he persists in teasing the cat. Then, one day he begins chasing the cat but the cat turns and swipes a claw across the dog's face, leaving him with a painful gash on his nose. The final result is that the dog stops chasing the cat.

TRAINING EQUIPMENT

Collar and Lead
For a Shar Pei the collar and lead that you use for training must be one with which you are easily able to work, not too heavy for the dog and perfectly safe.

Treats
Have a bag of treats on hand. Something nutritious and easy to swallow works best. Use a soft treat, a chunk of cheese or a piece of cooked chicken rather than a dry biscuit. By the time the dog has finished chewing a dry treat, he will forget why he is being rewarded in the first place! Using food rewards will not teach a dog to beg at the table—the only way to teach a dog to beg at the table is to give him food from the table. In training, rewarding the dog with a food treat will help him associate praise and the treats with learning new behaviours that obviously please his owner.

TRAINING BEGINS: ASK THE DOG A QUESTION
In order to teach your dog anything, you must first get his attention. After all, he cannot learn anything if he is looking away from you with his mind on something else.

To get his attention, ask him, 'School?' and immediately walk over to him and give him a treat as you tell him 'Good dog.' Wait a minute or two and repeat the routine, this time with a treat in your hand as you approach within a foot of the dog. Do not go directly to him, but stop about a foot short of him and hold out the treat as you ask, 'School?' He will see you approaching with a treat in your hand and most likely begin walking toward you. As you meet, give him the treat and praise again.

The third time, ask the question, have a treat in your hand and walk only a short distance toward the dog so that he must walk almost all the way to you. As he reaches you, give him the treat and praise again.

> **CONSISTENCY PAYS OFF**
>
> Dogs need consistency in their feeding schedule, exercise and toilet breaks and in the verbal commands you use. If you use 'Stay' on Monday and 'Stay here, please' on Tuesday, you will confuse your dog. Don't demand perfect behaviour during training classes and then let him have the run of the house the rest of the day. Above all, lavish praise on your pet consistently every time he does something right. The more he feels he is pleasing you, the more willing he will be to learn.

By this time, the dog will probably be getting the idea that if he pays attention to you, especially when you ask that question, it will pay off in treats and enjoyable activities for him. In other words, he learns that 'school' means doing great things with you that are fun and result in positive attention for him.

Remember that the dog does not understand your verbal language; he only recognises sounds. Your question translates to a series of sounds for him, and those sounds become the signal to go to you and pay attention; if he does, he will get to interact with you plus receive treats and praise.

THE BASIC COMMANDS

Teaching Sit

Now that you have the dog's attention, attach his lead and hold it in your left hand and a food treat in your right. Place your food hand at the dog's nose and let him lick the treat but not take it from you. Say 'Sit' and slowly raise your food hand from in front of the dog's nose up over his head so that he is looking at the ceiling. As he bends his head upward, he will have to bend his knees to maintain his balance. As he bends his knees, he will assume a sit position. At that point, release the food treat and praise lavishly with comments such as 'Good dog! Good sit!,' etc. Remember to always praise enthusiastically, because dogs relish verbal praise from their owners and feel so proud of themselves whenever they accomplish a behaviour.

> **HELPING PAWS**
>
> Your dog may not be the next Lassie, but every pet has the potential to do some tricks well. Identify his natural talents and hone them. Is your dog always happy and upbeat? Teach him to wag his tail or give you his paw on command. Real homebodies can be trained to do household chores, such as carrying dirty washing or retrieving the morning paper.

Housebreaking and Training

You will not use food forever in getting the dog to obey your commands. Food is only used to teach new behaviours, and once the dog knows what you want when you give a specific command, you will wean him off the food treats but still maintain the verbal praise. After all, you will always have your voice with you, and there will be many times when you have no food rewards but expect the dog to obey.

Teaching Down

Teaching the down exercise is easy when you understand how the dog perceives the down position, and it is very difficult when you do not. Dogs perceive the down position as a submissive one, therefore teaching the down exercise using a forceful method can sometimes make the dog develop such a fear of the down that he either runs away when you say 'Down' or he attempts to snap at the person who tries to force him down.

Have the dog sit close alongside your left leg, facing in the same direction as you are. Hold the lead in your left hand and a food treat in your right. Now place your left hand lightly on the top of the dog's shoulders where they meet above the spinal cord. Do not

> **HOW TO WEAN THE 'TREAT HOG'**
>
> If you have trained your dog by rewarding him with a treat each time he performs a command, he may soon decide that without the treat, he won't sit, stay or come. The best way to fix this problem is to start asking your dog to do certain commands twice before being rewarded. Slowly increase the number of commands given and then vary the number: three sits and a treat one day, five sits for a biscuit the next day. Your dog will soon realise that there is no set number of sits before he gets his reward, and he'll likely do it the first time you ask in the hope of being rewarded sooner rather than later.

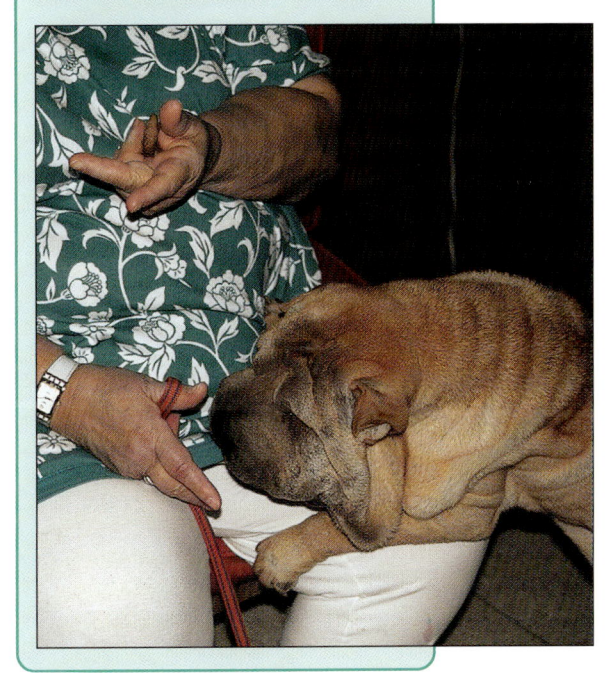

A well-trained Shar Pei is a pleasure to own and to meet. Owners should acknowledge a civic obligation to train their dogs to be upright canine citizens.

> **DOUBLE JEOPARDY**
> A dog in jeopardy never lies down. He stays alert on his feet because instinct tells him that he may have to run away or fight for his survival. Therefore, if a dog feels threatened or anxious, he will not lie down. Consequently, it is important to have the dog calm and relaxed as he learns the down exercise.

push down on the dog's shoulders; simply rest your left hand there so you can guide the dog to lie down close to your left leg rather than to swing away from your side when he drops.

Now place the food hand at the dog's nose, say 'Down' very softly (almost a whisper), and slowly lower the food hand to the dog's front feet. When the food hand reaches the floor, begin moving it forward along the floor in front of the dog. Keep talking softly to the dog, saying things like, 'Do you want this treat? You can do this, good dog.' Your reassuring tone of voice will help calm the dog as he tries to follow the food hand in order to get the treat.

When the dog's elbows touch the floor, release the food and praise softly. Try to get the dog to maintain that down position for several seconds before you let him sit up again. The goal here is to get the dog to settle down and not feel threatened in the down position.

> **THE GOLDEN RULE**
> The golden rule of dog training is simple. For each 'question' (command), there is only one correct answer (reaction). One command = one reaction. Keep practising the command until the dog reacts correctly without hesitating. Be repetitive but not monotonous. Dogs get bored just as people do!

Housebreaking and Training

TEACHING STAY

It is easy to teach the dog to stay in either a sit or a down position. Again, we use food and praise during the teaching process as we help the dog to understand exactly what it is that we are expecting him to do.

To teach the sit/stay, start with the dog sitting on your left side as before and hold the lead in your left hand. Have a food treat in your right hand and place your food hand at the

FETCH!

Play fetch games with your puppy in an enclosed area where he can retrieve his toy and bring it back to you. Always use a toy or object designated just for this purpose. Never use a shoe, stocking or other item he may later confuse with those in your wardrobe or underneath your chair.

THE STUDENT'S STRESS TEST

During training sessions you must be able to recognise signs of stress in your dog such as:
- tucking his tail between his legs
- lowering his head
- shivering or trembling
- standing completely still or running away
- panting and/or salivating
- avoiding eye contact
- flattening his ears back
- urinating submissively
- rolling over and lifting a leg
- grinning or baring teeth
- aggression when restrained

If your four-legged student displays these signs he may just be nervous or intimidated. The training session may have been too lengthy with not enough praise and affirmation. Stop for the day and try again tomorrow.

dog's nose. Say 'Stay' and step out on your right foot to stand directly in front of the dog, toe to toe, as he licks and nibbles the treat. Be sure to keep his head facing upward to maintain the sit position. Count to five and then swing around to stand next to the dog again with him on your left. As soon as you get back to the original position, release the food and praise lavishly.

To teach the down/stay, do the down as previously described. As soon as the dog lies down, say 'Stay' and step

> **KEEP SMILING**
> Never train your dog, puppy or adult, when you are angry or in a sour mood. Dogs are very sensitive to human feelings, especially anger, and if your dog senses that you are angry or upset, he will connect your anger with his training and learn to resent or fear his training sessions.

out on your right foot just as you did in the sit/stay. Count to five and then return to stand beside the dog with him on your left side. Release the treat and praise as always.

Within a week or ten days, you can begin to add a bit of distance between you and your dog when you leave him. When you do, use your left hand open with the palm facing the dog as a stay signal, much the same as the hand signal a constable uses to stop traffic at an intersection. Hold the food treat in your right hand as before, but this time the food is not touching the dog's nose. He will watch the food hand and quickly learn that he is going to get that treat as soon as you return to his side.

When you can stand 1 metre away from your dog for 30 seconds, you can then begin building time and distance in both stays. Eventually, the dog can be expected to remain in the stay position for prolonged periods of time until you return to him or call him to you. Always praise lavishly when he stays.

Teaching Come

If you make teaching 'come' an exciting experience, you should never have a 'student' that does not love the game or that fails to come when called. The secret, it seems, is never to teach the word 'come.'

At times when an owner most wants his dog to come when called, the owner is likely to be upset or anxious and he allows these feelings to come through in the tone of his voice when he calls his dog. Hearing that desperation in his owner's voice, the dog fears the results of going to him and therefore

> **DID YOU KNOW?**
> Occasionally, a dog and owner who have not attended formal classes have been able to earn entry-level titles by obtaining competition rules and regulations from a local kennel club and practising on their own to a degree of perfection. Obtaining the higher level titles, however, almost always requires extensive training under the tutelage of experienced instructors. In addition, the more difficult levels require more specialised equipment whereas the lower levels do not.

Housebreaking and Training

> **PLAN TO PLAY**
> The puppy should also have regular play and exercise sessions when he is with you or a family member. Exercise for a very young puppy can consist of a short walk around the house or garden. Playing can include fetching games with a large ball or a special raggy. (All puppies teethe and need soft things upon which to chew.) Remember to restrict play periods to indoors within his living area (the family room, for example) until he is completely housetrained.

either disobeys outright or runs in the opposite direction. The secret, therefore, is to teach the dog a game and, when you want him to come to you, simply play the game. It is practically a no-fail solution!

To begin, have several members of your family take a few food treats and each go into a different room in the house. Take turns calling the dog, and each person should celebrate the dog's finding him with a treat and lots of happy praise. When a person calls the dog, he is actually inviting the dog to find him and get a treat as a reward for 'winning.'

A few turns of the 'Where are you?' game and the dog will understand that everyone is playing the game and that each person has a big celebration awaiting his success at locating them. Once he learns to love the game, simply calling out 'Where are you?' will bring him running from wherever he is when he hears that all-important question.

The come command is recognised as one of the most important things to teach a dog, but there are trainers who work with thousands of dogs and never teach the actual word

Growing up with a Shar Pei has many rewards. Properly socialised, Shar Pei treat children like their own and make trustworthy nannies.

> **'WHERE ARE YOU?'**
> When calling the dog, do not say 'Come.' Say things like, 'Rover, where are you? See if you can find me! I have a biscuit for you!' Keep up a constant line of chatter with coaxing sounds and frequent questions such as, 'Where are you?' The dog will learn to follow the sound of your voice to locate you and receive his reward.

> **'COME'... BACK**
> Never call your dog to come to you for a correction or scold him when he reaches you. That is the quickest way to turn a 'Come' command into 'Go away fast!' Dogs think only in the present tense, and your dog will connect the scolding with coming to you, not with the misbehaviour of a few moments earlier.

'Come.' Yet these dogs will race to respond to a person who uses the dog's name followed by 'Where are you?' For example, a woman has a 12-year-old companion dog who went blind, but who never fails to locate her owner when asked, 'Where are you?'

Children, in particular, love to play this game with their dogs. Children can hide in smaller places like a shower or bath, behind a bed or under a table. The dog needs to work a little bit harder to find these hiding places, but when he does he loves to celebrate with a treat and a tussle with a favourite youngster.

TEACHING HEEL

Heeling means that the dog walks beside the owner without pulling. It takes time and patience on the owner's part to succeed at teaching the dog that he (the owner) will not proceed unless the dog is walking calmly beside him. Pulling out ahead on the lead is definitely not acceptable.

Begin by holding the lead in your left hand as the dog sits beside your left leg. Move the loop end of the lead to your right hand but keep your left hand short on the lead so it keeps the dog in close next to you.

Say 'Heel' and step forward on your left foot. Keep the dog close to you and take three steps. Stop and have the dog sit next to you in what we now call the 'heel position.' Praise verbally, but do not touch the dog. Hesitate a moment and begin again with 'Heel,' taking three steps and stopping, at which point the dog is told to sit again.

Your goal here is to have the dog walk those three steps

Housebreaking and Training

> **TUG OF WALK?**
> If you begin teaching the heel by taking long walks and letting the dog pull you along, he misinterprets this action as an acceptable form of taking a walk. When you pull back on the lead to counteract his pulling, he reads that tug as a signal to pull even harder!

without pulling on the lead. Once he will walk calmly beside you for three steps without pulling, increase the number of steps you take to five. When he will walk politely beside you while you take five steps, you can increase the length of your walk to ten steps. Keep increasing the length of your stroll until the dog will walk quietly beside you without pulling as long as you want him to heel. When you stop heeling, indicate to the dog that the exercise is over by verbally praising as you pet him and say 'OK, good dog.' The 'OK' is used as a release word meaning that the exercise is finished and the dog is free to relax.

If you are dealing with a dog who insists on pulling you around, simply 'put on your brakes' and stand your ground until the dog realises that the two of you are not going anywhere until he is beside you and moving at your pace, not his. It may take some time just standing there to convince the dog that you are the leader and you will be the one to decide on the direction and speed of your travel.

Each time the dog looks up at you or slows down to give a slack lead between the two of you, quietly praise him and say, 'Good heel. Good dog.' Eventually, the dog will begin to respond and within a few days he will be walking politely beside you without pulling on the lead. At first, the training sessions should be kept short and very positive; soon the dog will be able to walk nicely with you for increasingly longer

One of the most important lessons for the show-bound puppy is the heel. Show dogs must be able to heel on command to demonstrate proper gait in the show ring.

> **HEELING WELL**
> Teach your dog to HEEL in an enclosed area. Once you think the dog will obey reliably and you want to attempt advanced obedience exercises such as off-lead heeling, test him in a fenced-in area so he cannot run away.

> **TRAINING TIP**
> If you are walking your dog and he suddenly stops and looks straight into your eyes, ignore him. Pull the leash and lead him into the direction you want to walk.

distances. Remember also to give the dog free time and the opportunity to run and play when you have finished heel practice.

WEANING OFF FOOD IN TRAINING
Food is used in training new behaviours. Once the dog understands what behaviour goes with a specific command, it is time to start weaning him off the food treats. At first, give a treat after each exercise. Then, start to give a treat only after every other exercise. Mix up the times when you offer a food reward and the times when you only offer praise so that the dog will never know when he is going to receive both food and praise and when he is going to receive only praise. This is called a variable ratio reward system and it proves successful because there is always the chance that the owner will produce a treat, so the dog never

These two adult Shar Pei exhibit the proper intelligent expression for the breed. When socialised and trained, Shar Pei prove to be intense obedience students.

Housebreaking and Training

stops trying for that reward. No matter what, ALWAYS give verbal praise.

OBEDIENCE CLASSES

It is a good idea to enrol in an obedience class if one is available in your area. If yours is a show dog, ringcraft classes would be more appropriate. Many areas have dog clubs that offer basic obedience training as well as preparatory classes for obedience competition. There are also local dog trainers who offer similar classes.

At obedience trials, dogs can earn titles at various levels of competition. The beginning levels of competition include basic behaviours such as sit, down, heel, etc. The more advanced levels of competition include jumping, retrieving, scent discrimination and signal work. The advanced levels require a dog and owner to put a lot of time and effort into their training and the titles that can be earned at these levels of competition are very prestigious.

OTHER ACTIVITIES FOR LIFE

Whether a dog is trained in the structured environment of a class or alone with his owner at home, there are many activities that can bring fun and rewards to both owner and dog once they have mastered basic control.

Teaching the dog to help out around the home, in the garden or on the farm provides great satisfaction to both dog and owner. In addition, the dog's help makes life a little easier for his owner and raises his stature as a valued companion to his

> **SAFETY FIRST**
> While it may seem that the most important things to your dog are eating, sleeping and chewing the upholstery on your furniture, his first concern is actually safety. The domesticated dogs we keep as companions have the same pack instinct as their ancestors who ran free thousands of years ago. Because of this pack instinct, your dog wants to know that he and his pack are not in danger of being harmed, and that his pack has a strong, capable leader. You must establish yourself as the leader early on in your relationship. That way your dog will trust that you will take care of him and the pack, and he will accept your commands without question.

> **OBEDIENCE SCHOOL**
> A basic obedience beginner's class usually lasts for six to eight weeks. Dog and owner attend an hour-long lesson once a week and practise for a few minutes, several times a day, each day at home. If done properly, the whole procedure will result in a well-mannered dog and an owner who delights in living with a pet that is eager to please and enjoys doing things with his owner.

> **OBEDIENCE SCHOOL**
> Taking your dog to an obedience school may be the best investment in time and money you can ever make. You will enjoy the benefits for the lifetime of your dog and you will have the opportunity to meet people with your similar expectations for companion dogs.

family. It helps give the dog a purpose by occupying his mind and providing an outlet for his energy.

Backpacking is an exciting and healthy activity that the dog can be taught without assistance from more than his owner. The exercise of walking and climbing is good for man and dog alike, and the bond that they develop together is priceless.

If you are interested in participating in organised competition with your Shar Pei, there are activities other than obedience in which you and your dog can become involved. Agility is a popular sport where dogs run through an obstacle course that includes various jumps, tunnels and other exercises to test the dog's speed and coordination. The owners run beside their dogs to give commands and to guide them through the course. Although competitive, the focus is on fun—it's fun to do, fun to watch and great exercise.

> **FEAR AGGRESSION**
> Pups who are subjected to physical abuse during training commonly end up with behavioural problems as adults. One common result of abuse is fear aggression, in which a dog will lash out, bare his teeth, snarl and finally bite someone by whom he feels threatened. For example, your daughter may be playing with the dog one afternoon. As they play hide-and-seek, she backs the dog into a corner, and as she attempts to tease him playfully, he bites her hand. Examine the cause of this behaviour. Did your daughter ever hit the dog? Did someone who resembles your daughter hit or scream at the dog? Fortunately, fear aggression is relatively easy to correct. Have your daughter engage in only positive activities with the dog, such as feeding, petting and walking. She should not give any corrections or negative feedback. If the dog still growls or cowers away from her, allow someone else to accompany them. After approximately one week, the dog should feel that he can rely on her for many positive things, and he will also be prevented from reacting fearfully towards anyone who might resemble her.

Housebreaking and Training

Shar Pei make loving and affectionate home companions. This well-kept Shar Pei seems to rule the roost in his home.

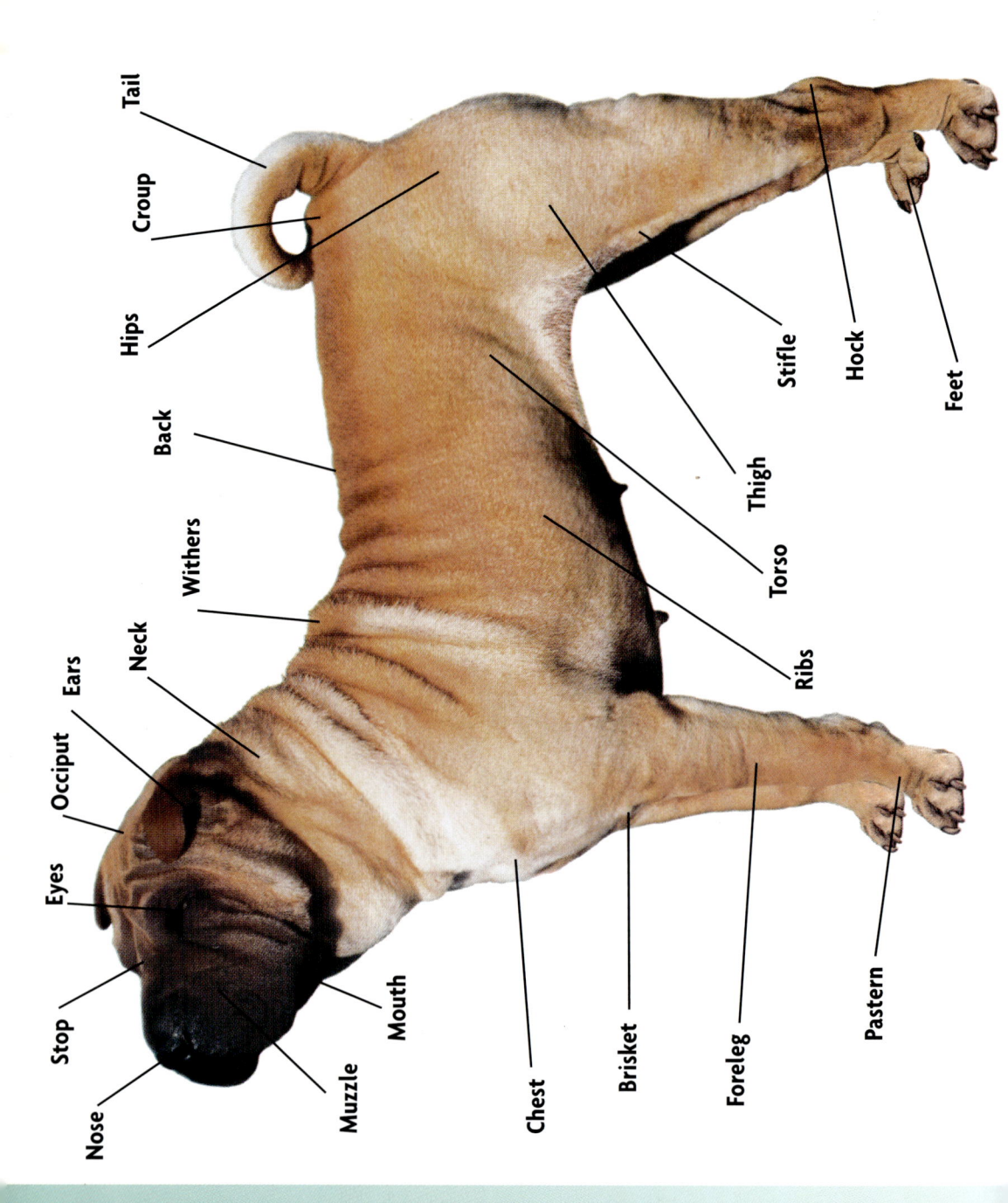

Physical Structure of the Shar Pei

Health Care of Your
SHAR PEI

Dogs suffer many of the same physical illnesses as people. They might even share many of the same psychological problems. Since people usually know more about human diseases than canine maladies, many of the terms used in this chapter will be familiar but not necessarily those used by veterinary surgeons. We will use the term *x-ray*, instead of the more acceptable term *radiograph*. We will also use the familiar term symptoms even though dogs don't have *symptoms*, which are verbal descriptions of the patient's feelings; dogs have *clinical signs*. Since dogs can't speak, we have to look for clinical signs...but we still use the term symptoms in this book.

As a general rule, medicine is practised. That term is not arbitrary. Medicine is a constantly changing art as we learn more and more about genetics, electronic aids (like CAT scans) and daily laboratory advances. There are many dog maladies, like canine hip dysplasia, which are not universally treated in the same manner. Some veterinary surgeons opt for surgery more often than others do.

SELECTING A VETERINARY SURGEON

Your selection of a veterinary surgeon should not be based upon personality (as most are) but upon their convenience to your home. You want a vet who is close because you might have emergencies or need to make multiple visits for treatments. You want a vet who has services that you might require such as tattooing and grooming, as well as sophisticated pet supplies and a good reputation for ability and

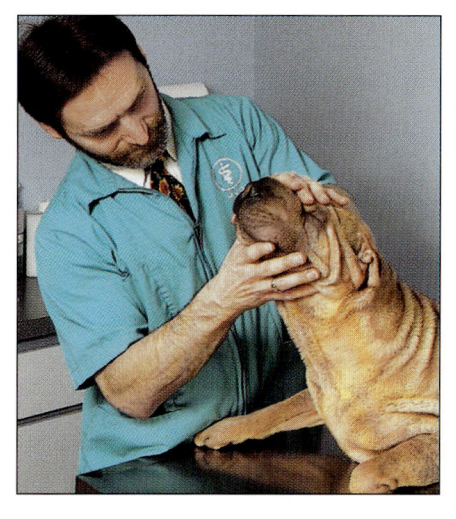

> Your Shar Pei's best friend might very well be the veterinary surgeon who supervises the dog's diet, vaccination schedule and general health and well-being.

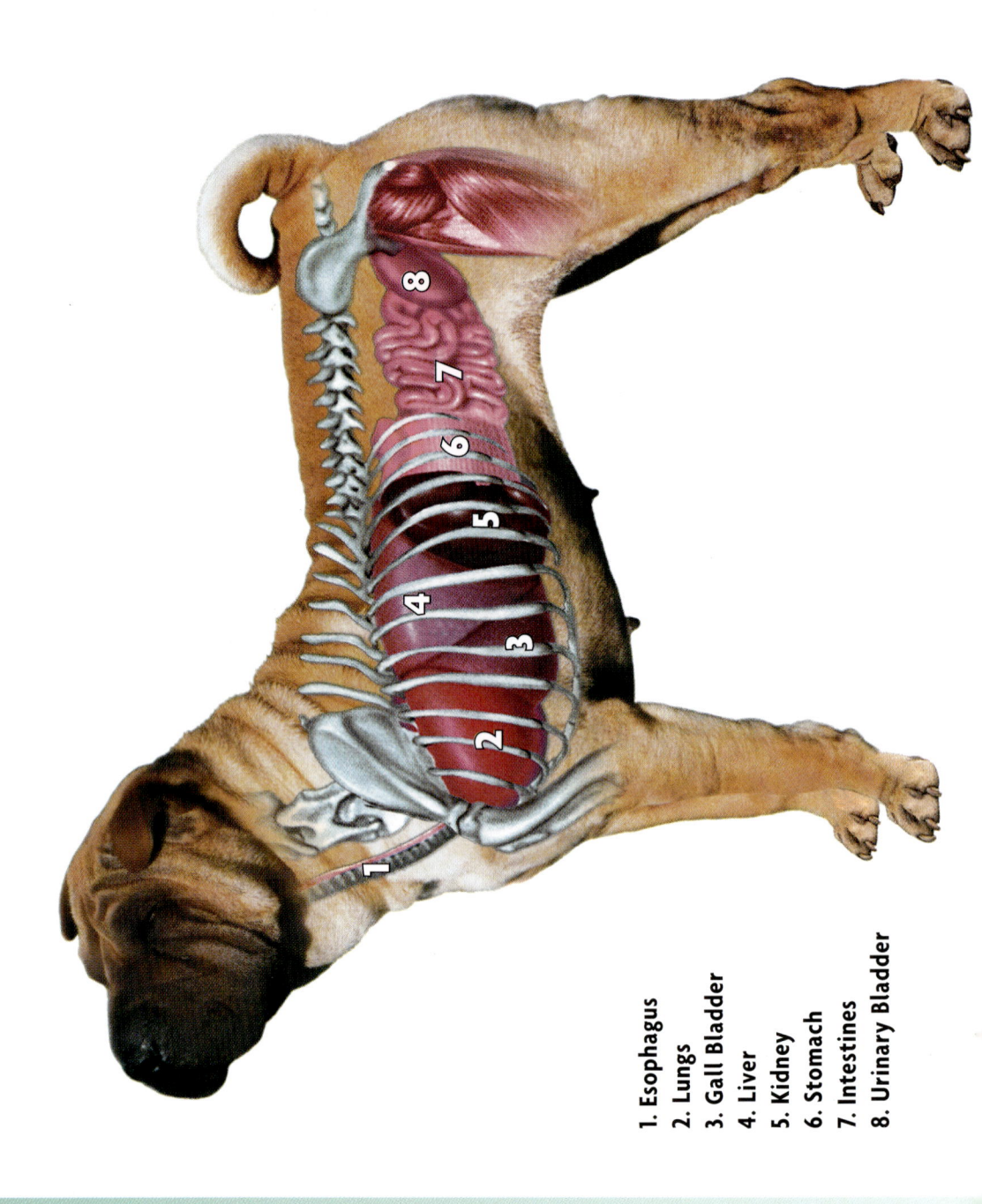

1. Esophagus
2. Lungs
3. Gall Bladder
4. Liver
5. Kidney
6. Stomach
7. Intestines
8. Urinary Bladder

Internal Organs of the Shar Pei

Health Care

responsiveness. There is nothing more frustrating than having to wait a day or more to get a response from your veterinary surgeon.

All veterinary surgeons are licensed and their diplomas and/or certificates should be displayed in their waiting rooms. There are, however, many veterinary specialities that usually require further studies and internships. There are specialists in heart problems (veterinary cardiologists), skin problems (veterinary dermatologists), teeth and gum problems (veterinary dentists), eye problems (veterinary ophthalmologists) and x-rays (veterinary radiologists), as well as vets who have specialities in bones, muscles or other organs. Most veterinary surgeons do routine surgery such as neutering, stitching up wounds and docking tails for those breeds in which such is required for show purposes. When the problem affecting your dog is serious, it is not unusual or impudent to get another medical opinion, although in Britain you are obliged to advise the vets concerned about this. You might also want to compare costs amongst several veterinary surgeons. Sophisticated health care and veterinary services can be very costly. It is not infrequent that important decisions are based upon financial considerations.

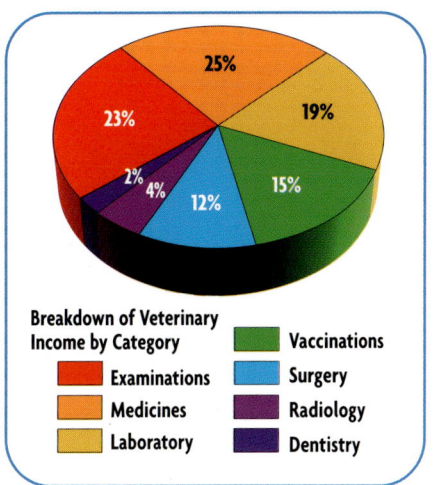

Breakdown of Veterinary Income by Category
- Examinations: 23%
- Medicines: 25%
- Laboratory: 19%
- Vaccinations: 15%
- Surgery: 12%
- Radiology: 4%
- Dentistry: 2%

A typical American vet's income, categorised according to services provided. This survey dealt with small-animal practices.

PREVENTATIVE MEDICINE

It is much easier, less costly and more effective to practise preventative medicine than to fight bouts of illness and disease. Properly bred puppies come from parents that were selected based upon their genetic disease profile. Their mothers should have been vaccinated, free of all internal and external parasites and properly nourished. For these reasons, a visit to the veterinary surgeon who cared for the dam is recommended. The dam can pass on disease resistance to her puppies, which can last for eight to ten weeks. She can also pass on parasites and many infections. That's why

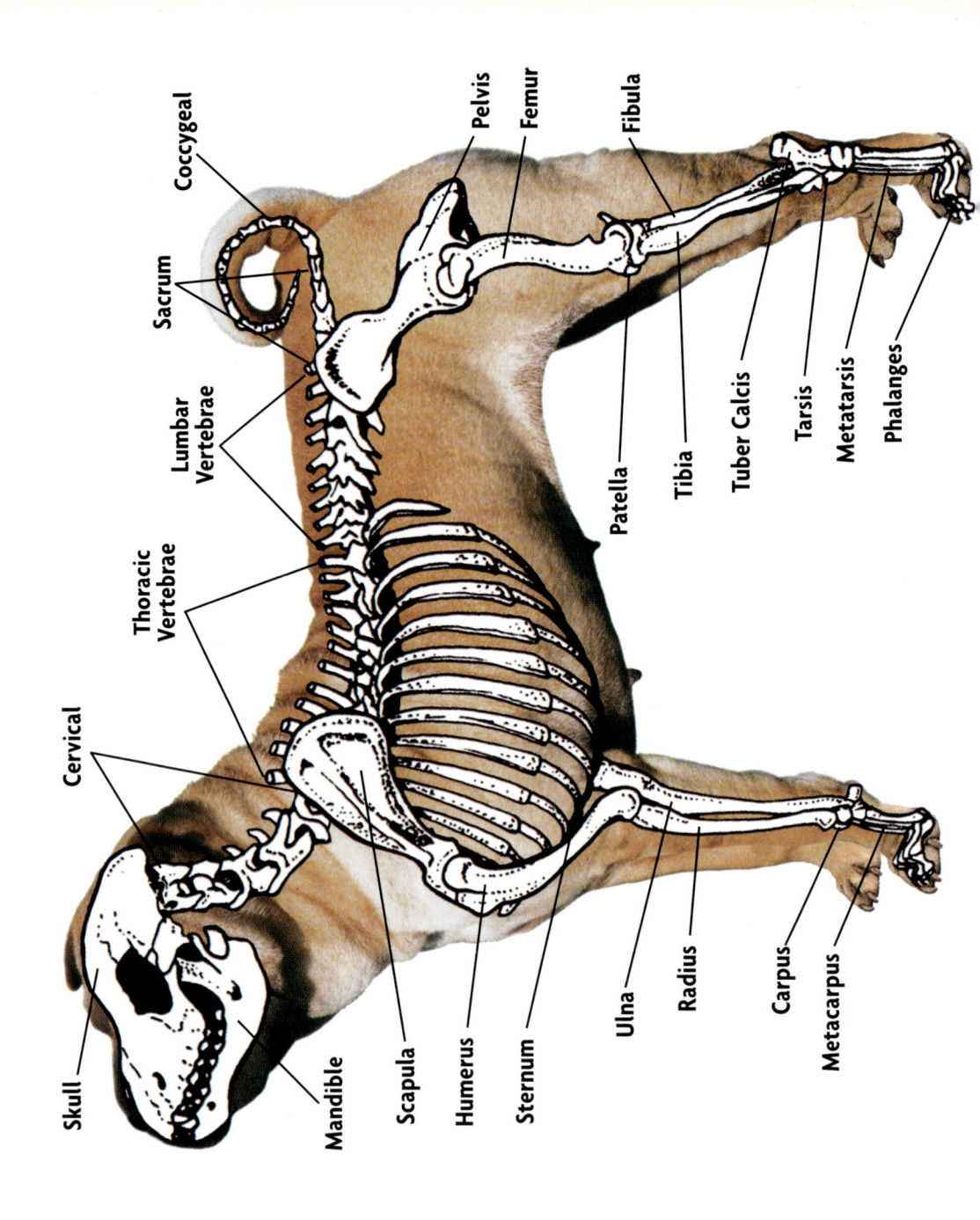

Skeletal Structure of the Shar Pei

Health Care

you should visit the veterinary surgeon who cared for the dam.

Vaccination Scheduling

Most vaccinations are given by injection and should only be done by a veterinary surgeon. Both he and you should keep a record of the date of the injection, the identification of the vaccine and the amount given. Some vets give a first vaccination at eight weeks, but most dog breeders prefer the course not to commence until about ten weeks because of negating any antibodies passed on by the dam. The vaccination scheduling is usually based on a 15-day cycle. You must take your vet's advice regarding when to vaccinate as this may differ according to the vaccine used. Most vaccinations immunize your puppy against viruses.

The usual vaccines contain immunizing doses of several different viruses such as distemper, parvovirus, parainfluenza and hepatitis. There are other vaccines available when the puppy is at risk. You should rely upon professional advice. This is especially true for the booster-shot programme. Most vaccination programmes require a booster when the puppy is a year old and once a year thereafter. In some cases, circumstances may require

DENTAL HEALTH
A dental examination is in order when the dog is between six months and one year of age so any permanent teeth that have erupted incorrectly can be corrected. It is important to begin a brushing routine, preferably using a two-sided brushing technique, whereby both sides of the tooth are brushed at the same time. Durable nylon and safe edible chews should be a part of your puppy's arsenal for good health, good teeth and pleasant breath. The vast majority of dogs three to four years old and older have diseases of the gums from lack of dental attention. Using the various types of dental chews can be very effective in controlling dental plaque.

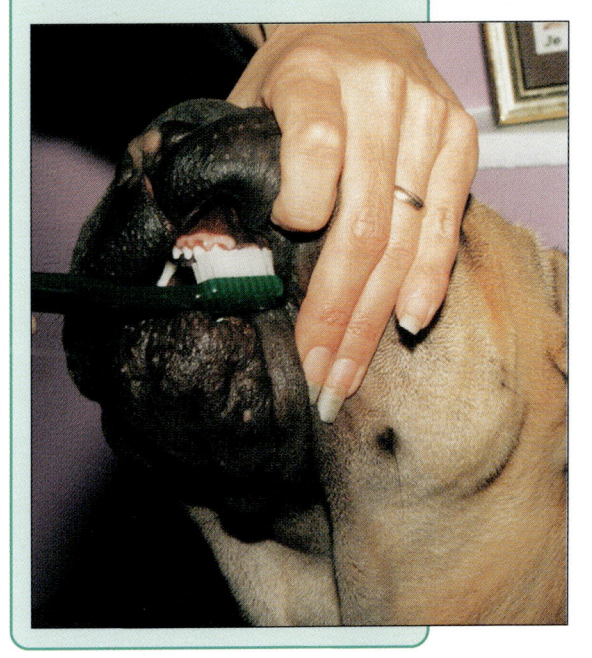

122 • *Shar Pei*

Normal dog hairs enlarged 200 times natural size. The cuticle (outer covering) is clean and healthy. Unlike human hairs, which grow from the base, dog hairs grow from the end, as is shown in the inset. Scanning electron micrographs by Dr Dennis Kunkel, University of Hawaii.

S. E. M. by Dr Dennis Kunkel, University of Hawaii

Health Care

> **VACCINE ALLERGIES**
> Vaccines do not work all the time. Sometimes dogs are allergic to them and many times the antibodies, which are supposed to be stimulated by the vaccine, just are not produced. You should keep your dog in the veterinary clinic for an hour after it is vaccinated to be sure there are no allergic reactions.

more or less frequent immunizations. Kennel cough, more formally known as tracheobronchitis, is treated with a vaccine that is sprayed into the dog's nostrils. Kennel cough is usually included in routine vaccination, but this is often not so effective as for other major diseases.

WEANING TO FIVE MONTHS OLD
Puppies should be weaned by the time they are about two months old. A puppy that remains for at least eight weeks with its mother and littermates usually adapts better to other dogs and people later in its life.

Some new owners have their puppy examined by a veterinary surgeon immediately, which is a good idea. Vaccination programmes usually begin when the puppy is very young.

The puppy will have its teeth examined and have its skeletal conformation and general health checked prior to certification by the veterinary surgeon. Puppies in certain breeds have problems with their kneecaps, cataracts and other eye problems, heart murmurs and undescended testicles. They may also have personality problems and your veterinary surgeon might have training in temperament evaluation.

> **MORE THAN VACCINES**
> Vaccinations help prevent your new puppy from contracting diseases, but they do not cure them. Proper nutrition as well as parasite control keep your dog healthy and less susceptible to many dangerous diseases. Remember that your dog depends on you to ensure his well-being.

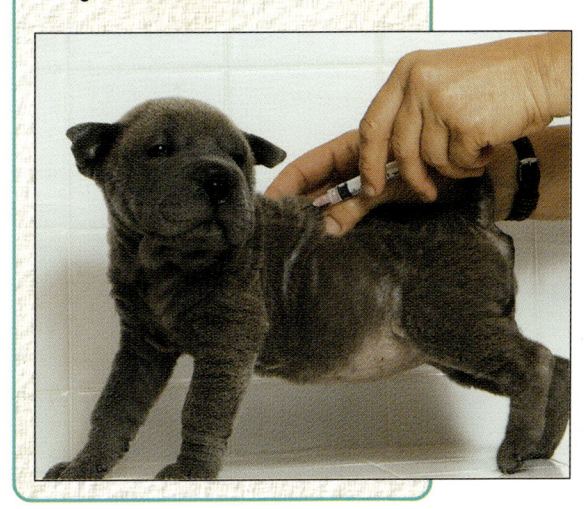

HEALTH AND VACCINATION SCHEDULE

Age in Weeks:	6th	8th	10th	12th	14th	16th	20-24th	1 yr
Worm Control	✔	✔	✔	✔	✔	✔	✔	
Neutering								✔
Heartworm*		✔		✔		✔	✔	
Parvovirus	✔		✔		✔		✔	✔
Distemper		✔		✔		✔		✔
Hepatitis		✔		✔		✔		✔
Leptospirosis								✔
Parainfluenza	✔		✔		✔			✔
Dental Examination		✔					✔	✔
Complete Physical		✔					✔	✔
Coronavirus				✔			✔	✔
Kennel Cough	✔							
Hip Dysplasia								✔
Rabies*							✔	

Vaccinations are not instantly effective. It takes about two weeks for the dog's immunization system to develop antibodies. Most vaccinations require annual booster shots. Your veterinary surgeon should guide you in this regard.

*Not applicable in the United Kingdom

FIVE TO TWELVE MONTHS OF AGE
Unless you intend to breed or show your dog, neutering the puppy at six months of age is recommended. Discuss this with your veterinary surgeon. Neutering has proven to be extremely beneficial to both male and female puppies. Besides eliminating the possibility of pregnancy, it inhibits (but does not prevent) breast cancer in bitches and prostate cancer in male dogs. Under no circumstances should a bitch be spayed prior to her first season.

Your veterinary surgeon should provide your puppy with a thorough dental evaluation at six months of age, ascertaining whether all the permanent teeth have erupted properly. A home dental care regimen should be initiated at six months, including brushing weekly and providing good dental devices (such as nylon bones). Regular dental care promotes healthy teeth, fresh breath and a longer life.

ONE TO SEVEN YEARS
Once a year, your grown dog

Health Care

should visit the vet for an examination and vaccination boosters. Some vets recommend blood tests, thyroid level check and dental evaluation to accompany these annual visits. A thorough clinical evaluation by the vet can provide critical background information for your dog. Blood tests are often performed at one year of age, and dental examinations around the third or fourth birthday. In the long run, quality preventative care for your pet can save money, teeth and lives.

SKIN PROBLEMS IN SHAR PEI

Veterinary surgeons are consulted by dog owners for skin problems more than any other group of diseases or maladies. For the Shar Pei, however, skin problems are the most common problem, primarily due to the breed's

DISEASE REFERENCE CHART

	What is it?	What causes it?	Symptoms
Leptospirosis	Severe disease that affects the internal organs; can be spread to people.	A bacterium, which is often carried by rodents, that enters through mucous membranes and spreads quickly throughout the body.	Range from fever, vomiting and loss of appetite in less severe cases to shock, irreversible kidney damage and possibly death in most severe cases.
Rabies	Potentially deadly virus that infects warm-blooded mammals. Not seen in United Kingdom.	Bite from a carrier of the virus, mainly wild animals.	1st stage: dog exhibits change in behaviour, fear. 2nd stage: dog's behaviour becomes more aggressive. 3rd stage: loss of coordination, trouble with bodily functions.
Parvovirus	Highly contagious virus, potentially deadly.	Ingestion of the virus, which is usually spread through the faeces of infected dogs.	Most common: severe diarrhoea. Also vomiting, fatigue, lack of appetite.
Kennel cough	Contagious respiratory infection.	Combination of types of bacteria and virus. Most common: *Bordetella bronchiseptica* bacteria and parainfluenza virus.	Chronic cough.
Distemper	Disease primarily affecting respiratory and nervous system.	Virus that is related to the human measles virus.	Mild symptoms such as fever, lack of appetite and mucous secretion progress to evidence of brain damage, 'hard pad.'
Hepatitis	Virus primarily affecting the liver.	Canine adenovirus type I (CAV-1). Enters system when dog breathes in particles.	Lesser symptoms include listlessness, diarrhoea, vomiting. More severe symptoms include 'blue-eye' (clumps of virus in eye).
Coronavirus	Virus resulting in digestive problems.	Virus is spread through infected dog's faeces.	Stomach upset evidenced by lack of appetite, vomiting, diarrhoea.

PARVO FOR THE COURSE

Canine parvovirus is a highly contagious disease that attacks puppies and older dogs. Spread through contact with infected faeces, parvovirus causes bloody diarrhoea, vomiting, heart damage, dehydration, shock and death. To prevent this tragedy, have your puppy begin his series of vaccinations at six to eight weeks. Be aware that the virus is easily spread and is carried on a dog's hair and feet, water bowls and other objects, as well as people's shoes and clothing.

characteristic wrinkles. Amongst the common skin ailments of Shar Pei are Shar Pei syndrome (or rash), demodectic mange, mucinosis, body fold dermatitis, seborrhea, as well as general irritation of the skin. Dogs' skin is almost as sensitive as human skin and both suffer almost the same ailments. (Though the occurrence of acne in dogs is rare!) For this reason, veterinary dermatology has developed into a speciality practised by many veterinary surgeons, many of whom are intimately acquainted with the Shar Pei.

Since many skin problems have visual symptoms that are almost identical, it requires the skill of an experienced veterinary dermatologist to identify and cure many of the more severe skin disorders. Pet shops sell many treatments for skin problems but most of the treatments are directed at symptoms and not the underlying problem(s). If your dog is suffering from a skin disorder, you should seek professional assistance as quickly as possible. As with all diseases, the earlier a problem is identified and treated, the more successful is the cure.

Parasite Bites

Many of us are allergic to insect bites. The bites itch, erupt and may even become infected. Dogs have the same reaction to fleas, ticks and/or mites. When an insect lands on you, you have the chance to whisk it away with your hand. Unfortunately, when your dog is bitten by a flea, tick or mite, it can only scratch it away or bite it. By the time the dog has been bitten, the parasite has done some of its damage. It may also have laid eggs to cause further problems in the near future. The itching from parasite bites is probably due to the saliva injected into the site when the parasite sucks the dog's blood.

Auto-Immune Skin Conditions

Auto-immune skin conditions are commonly referred to as

First Aid at a Glance

Burns
Place the affected area under cool water; use ice if only a small area is burnt.

Bee/Insect bites
Apply ice to relieve swelling; antihistamine dosed properly.

Animal bites
Clean any bleeding area; apply pressure until bleeding subsides; go to the vet.

Spider bites
Use cold compress and a pressurised pack to inhibit venom's spreading.

Antifreeze poisoning
Induce vomiting with hydrogen peroxide. Seek *immediate* veterinary help!

Fish hooks
Removal best handled by vet; hook must be cut in order to remove.

Snake bites
Pack ice around bite; contact vet quickly; identify snake for proper antivenin.

Car accident
Move dog from roadway with blanket; seek veterinary aid.

Shock
Calm the dog, keep him warm; seek immediate veterinary help.

Nosebleed
Apply cold compress to the nose; apply pressure to any visible abrasion.

Bleeding
Apply pressure above the area; treat wound by applying a cotton pack.

Heat stroke
Submerge dog in cold bath; cool down with fresh air and water; go to the vet.

Frostbite/Hypothermia
Warm the dog with a warm bath, electric blankets or hot water bottles.

Abrasions
Clean the wound and wash out thoroughly with fresh water; apply antiseptic.

!! **Remember: an injured dog may attempt to bite a helping hand from fear and confusion. Always muzzle the dog before trying to offer assistance.** !!

being allergic to yourself, while allergies are usually inflammatory reactions to an outside stimulus. Auto-immune diseases cause serious damage to the tissues that are involved.

The best known auto-immune disease is lupus, which affects people as well as dogs. The symptoms are variable and may affect the kidneys, bones, blood chemistry and skin. It can be fatal to both dogs and humans, though it is not thought to be transmissible. It is usually successfully treated with cortisone, prednisone or a similar corticosteroid, but extensive use of these drugs can have harmful side effects.

Excessive licking of a hot spot (acral lick) is treatable but not always curable. Usually the hot spot is on the hindquarters or forequarters.

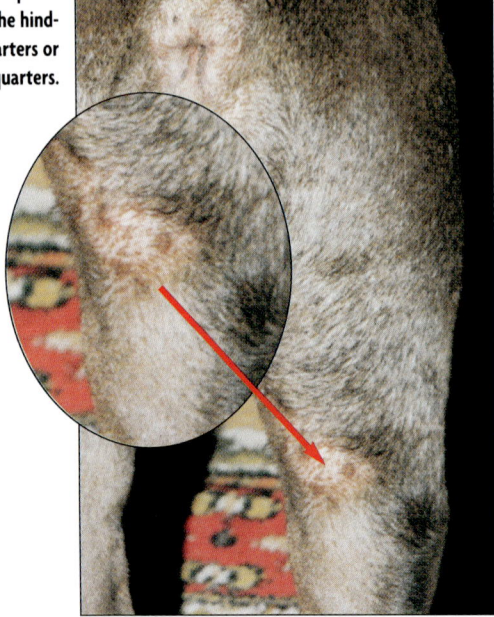

Hot Spots and Excessive Licking

The manifestation of the problem of excessive licking is the dog's tireless chewing at a specific area of the body, almost always the feet or paws. Shar Pei often suffer from soreness between their toes, and they lick so intensively that they remove the hair and skin. Owners who notice their dogs' biting and chewing at their extremities should have the vet determine the cause. Hot spots, or moist dermatitis, are common in coated breeds and often occur in the warmer months. These irritations often occur in the rear quarters, on the thigh or on the back where the tail curls. Hot spots are also caused by the dog's excessive licking for seemingly unexplained reasons. The vet should be consulted, as the area needs to be shaved, cleaned and anointed, usually accompanied by a corticosteroid injection and oral supplements.

Airborne Allergies

An interesting allergy is pollen allergy. Humans have hay fever, rose fever and other fevers with which they suffer during the pollinating season. Many dogs suffer the same allergies. When the pollen count is high, your dog might

Health Care

suffer but don't expect him to sneeze and have a runny nose like humans. Dogs react to pollen allergies the same way they react to fleas—they scratch and bite themselves.

Dogs, like humans, can be tested for allergens. Discuss the testing with your veterinary dermatologist.

FOOD PROBLEMS

FOOD ALLERGIES

Dogs are allergic to many foods that are best-sellers and highly recommended by breeders and veterinary surgeons. Changing the brand of food that you buy may not eliminate the problem if the element to which the dog

Fatty Risks

Any dog of any breed can suffer from obesity. Studies show that nearly 30 percent of our dogs are overweight, primarily from high caloric intake and low energy expenditure. The hound and gundog breeds are the most likely affected, and females are at a greater risk of obesity than males. Pet dogs that are neutered are twice as prone to obesity as intact, whole dogs.

Regardless of breed, your dog should have a visible 'waist' behind his rib cage and in front of the hind legs. There should be no fatty deposits on his hips or over his rump, and his abdomen should not be extended.

Veterinary specialists link obesity with respiratory problems, cardiac disease and liver dysfunction as well as low sperm count and abnormal oestrous cycles in breeding animals. Other complications include musculoskeletal disease (including arthritis), decreased immune competence, diabetes mellitus, hypothroidism, pancreatitis and dermatosis. Other studies have indicated that excess fat leads to heat stress, as obese dogs cannot regulate their body temperatures as well as normal-weight dogs.

Don't be discouraged if you discover that your dog has a heart problem or a complicated neurological condition requiring special attention. It is possible to tend to his special medical needs. Veterinary specialists focus on areas such as cardiology, neurology and oncology. Veterinary medical associations require rigorous training and experience before granting certification in a speciality. Consulting a specialist may offer you greater peace of mind when seeking treatment for your dog.

> **CARETAKER OF TEETH**
> You are your dog's caretaker and his dentist. Vets warn that plaque and tartar buildup on the teeth will damage the gums and allow bacteria to enter the dog's bloodstream, causing serious damage to the animal's vital organs. Studies show that over 50 percent of dogs have some form of gum disease before age three. Daily or weekly tooth cleaning (with a brush or soft gauze pad wipes) can add years to your dog's life.

is allergic is contained in the new brand.

Recognising a food allergy is difficult. Humans vomit or have rashes when they eat a food to which they are allergic. Dogs neither vomit nor (usually) develop a rash. They react in the same manner as they do to an airborne or flea allergy; they itch, scratch and bite, thus making the diagnosis extremely difficult. While pollen allergies and parasite bites are usually seasonal, food allergies are year-round problems.

FOOD INTOLERANCE

Food intolerance is the inability of the dog to completely digest certain foods. Puppies that may have done very well on their mother's milk may not do well on cow's milk. The rest of this food intolerance may be loose bowels, passing gas and stomach pains. These are the only obvious symptoms of food intolerance and that makes diagnosis difficult

TREATING FOOD PROBLEMS

It is possible to handle food allergies and food intolerance yourself. Put your dog on a diet that it has never had. Obviously if it has never eaten this new food it can't have been allergic or intolerant of it. Start with a single ingredient that is not in the dog's diet at the present time. Ingredients like chopped beef or fish are common in dogs' diets, so try something more exotic like rabbit, pheasant or even just vegetables. Keep the dog on

> **'P' STANDS FOR PROBLEM**
> Urinary tract disease is a serious condition that requires immediate medical attention. Symptoms include urinating in inappropriate places or the need to urinate frequently in small amounts. Urinary tract disease is most effectively treated with antibiotics. To help promote good urinary tract health, owners must always be sure that a constant supply of fresh water is available to their pets.

Health Care

> **DID YOU KNOW?**
> Your dog's protein needs are changeable. High activity level, stress, climate and other physical factors may require your dog to have more protein in his diet. Check with your veterinary surgeon.

this diet (with no additives) for a month. If the symptoms of food allergy or intolerance disappear, chances are your dog has a food allergy.

Don't think that the single ingredient cured the problem. You still must find a suitable diet and ascertain which ingredient in the old diet was objectionable. This is most easily done by adding ingredients to the new diet one at a time. Let the dog stay on the modified diet for a month before you add another ingredient. Eventually, you will determine the ingredient that caused the adverse reaction.

An alternative method is to carefully study the ingredients in the diet to which your dog is allergic or intolerant. Identify the main ingredient in this diet and eliminate the main ingredient by buying a different food that does not have that ingredient. Keep experimenting until the symptoms disappear after one month on the new diet.

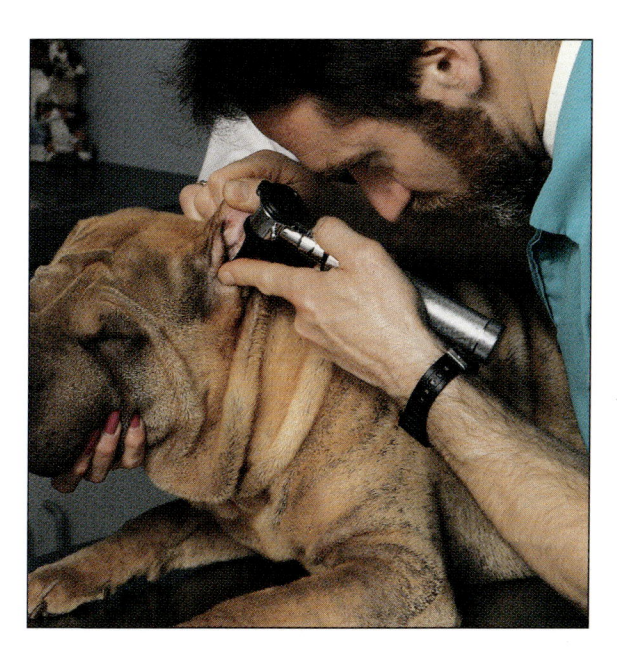

> **A SKUNKY PROBLEM**
> Have you noticed your dog dragging his rump along the floor? If so, it is likely that his anal sacs are impacted or possibly infected. The anal sacs are small pouches located on both sides of the anus under the skin and muscles. They are about the size and shape of a grape and contain a foul-smelling liquid. Their contents are usually emptied when the dog has a bowel movement, but if they are not emptied completely, they will impact, which will cause your dog a lot of pain. Fortunately, your veterinary surgeon can tend to this problem easily by draining the sacs for the dog. Be aware that your dog might also empty his anal sacs in cases of extreme fright.

The Shar Pei's ears are small and, thus, not well ventilated, making them susceptible to bacteria buildup and infection. You should check the ears regularly at home; any sign of a problem requires veterinary attention.

EXTERNAL PARASITES

Of all the problems to which dogs are prone, none is more well known and frustrating than fleas. Flea infestation is relatively simple to cure but difficult to prevent. Parasites that are harboured inside the body are a bit more difficult to eradicate but they are easier to control.

FLEAS

To control a flea infestation you have to understand the flea's life cycle. Fleas are often thought of as a summertime problem but centrally heated homes have changed the patterns and fleas can be found at any time of the year. The most effective method of flea control is a two-stage approach: one stage to kill the adult fleas, and the other to control the development of pre-adult fleas. Unfortunately, no single active ingredient is effective against all stages of the life cycle.

LIFE CYCLE STAGES

During its life, a flea will pass through four life stages: egg, larva, pupa and adult. The adult stage is the most visible and irritating stage of the flea life cycle and this is why the majority of flea-control products concentrate on this stage.

A scanning electron micrograph (S. E. M.) of a dog flea, *Ctenocephalides canis*.

Magnified head of a dog flea, *Ctenocephalides canis*.

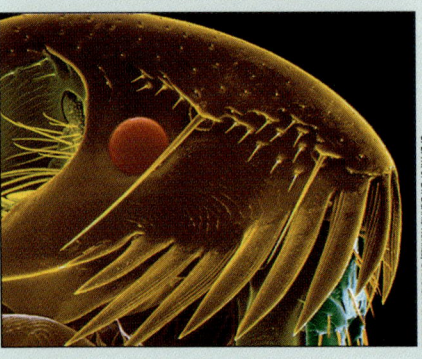

A Look at Fleas

Fleas have been around for millions of years and have adapted to changing host animals. They are able to go through a complete life cycle in less than one month or they can extend their lives to almost two years by remaining as pupae or cocoons. They do not need blood or any other food for up to 20 months.

They have been measured as being able to jump 300,000 times and can jump 150 times their length in any direction including straight up. Those are just a few of the reasons why they are so successful in infesting a dog!

Health Care

The fact is that adult fleas account for only 1% of the total flea population, and the other 99% exist in pre-adult stages, i.e. eggs, larvae and pupae. The pre-adult stages are barely visible to the naked eye.

The Life Cycle of the Flea

Eggs are laid on the dog, usually in quantities of about 20 or 30, several times a day. The female adult flea must have a blood meal before each egg-laying session. When first laid, the eggs will cling to the dog's fur, as the eggs are still moist. However, they will quickly dry out and fall from the dog, especially if the dog moves around or scratches. Many eggs will fall off in the dog's favourite area or an area in which he spends a lot of time, such as his bed.

Once the eggs fall from the dog onto the carpet or furniture, they will hatch into larvae. This takes from one to ten days. Larvae are not particularly mobile, and will usually travel only a few inches from where they hatch. However, they do have a tendency to move away from light and heavy traffic—under furniture and behind doors are common places to find high quantities of flea larvae.

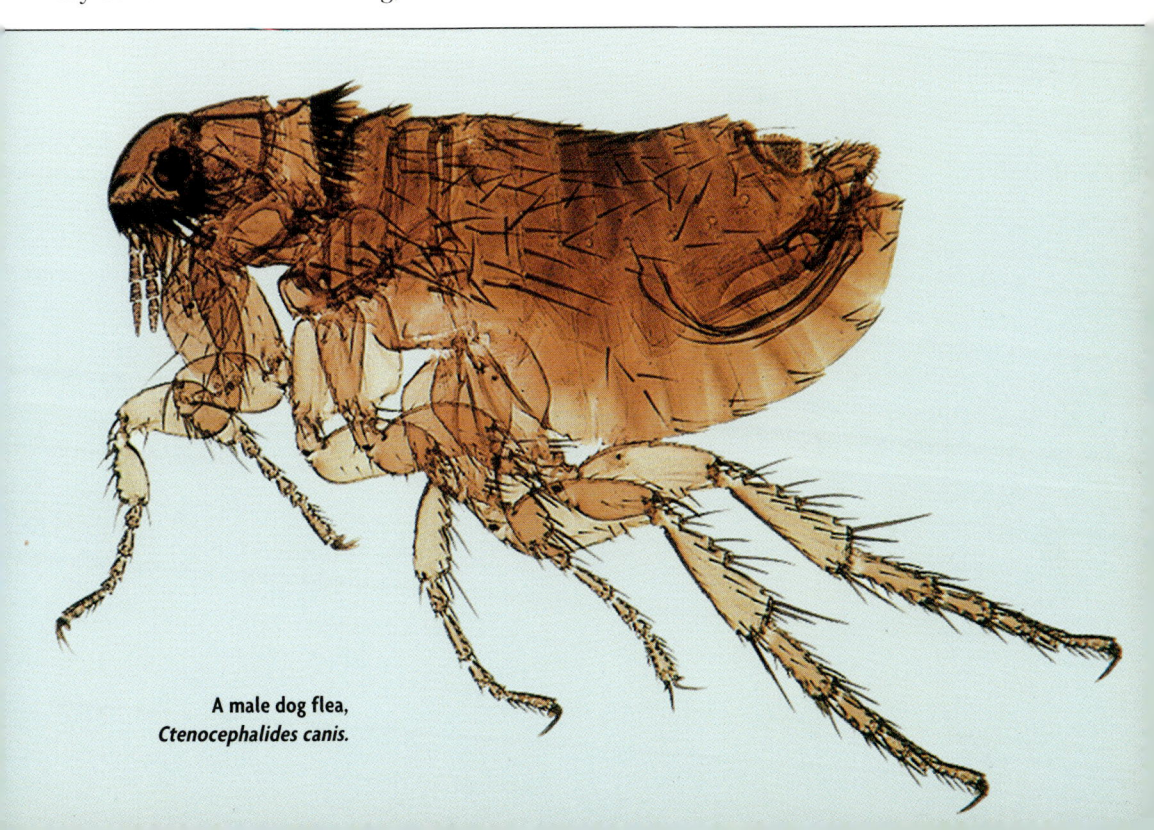

A male dog flea, *Ctenocephalides canis*.

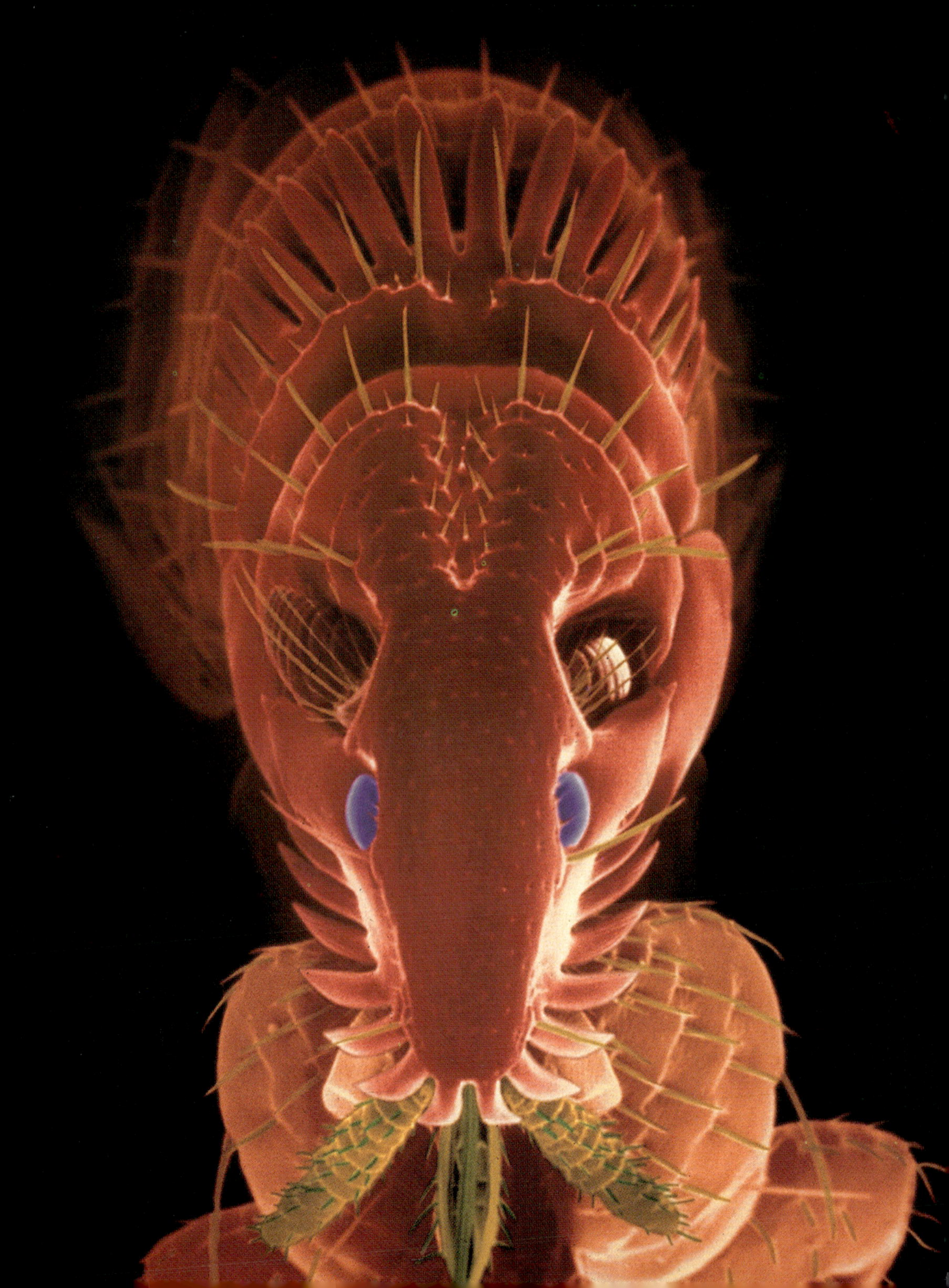

Health Care

The flea larvae feed on dead organic matter, including adult flea faeces, until they are ready to change into adult fleas. Fleas will usually remain as larvae for around seven days. After this period, the larvae will pupate into protective pupae. While inside the pupae, the larvae will undergo metamorphosis and change into adult fleas. This can take as little time as a few days, but the adult fleas can remain inside the pupae waiting to hatch for up to two years. The pupae are signalled to hatch by certain stimuli, such as physical pressure—the pupae's being stepped on, heat from an animal lying on the pupae or increased carbon dioxide levels and vibrations—indicating that a suitable host is available.

Once hatched, the adult flea must feed within a few days. Once the adult flea finds a host, it will not leave voluntarily. It only becomes dislodged by grooming or the host animal's scratching. The adult flea will remain on the host for the duration of its life unless forcibly removed.

> **DID YOU KNOW?**
> Never mix flea control products without first consulting your veterinary surgeon. Some products can become toxic when combined with others and can cause serious or fatal consequences.

> **DID YOU KNOW?**
> Flea-killers are poisonous. You should not spray these toxic chemicals on areas of a dog's body that he licks, on his genitals or on his face. Flea killers taken internally are a better answer, but check with your vet in case internal therapy is not advised for your dog.

TREATING THE ENVIRONMENT AND THE DOG

Treating fleas should be a two-pronged attack. First, the environment needs to be treated; this includes carpets and furniture, especially the dog's bedding and areas underneath furniture. The environment should be treated with a household spray containing an Insect Growth Regulator (IGR) and an insecticide to kill the adult fleas. Most IGRs are effective against eggs and larvae; they actually mimic the fleas' own hormones and stop the eggs and larvae from developing into adult fleas. There are currently no treatments available to attack the pupa stage of the life cycle, so the adult insecticide is used to kill the newly hatched adult fleas before they find a host. Most IGRs are active for many months, whilst adult insecticides are only active for a few days.

When treating with a household spray, it is a good idea to vacuum before applying the

Opposite page: A scanning electron micrograph of a dog or cat flea, Ctenocephalides, magnified more than 100x. This image has been colorized for effect.

The Life Cycle of the Flea

Eggs

Larva

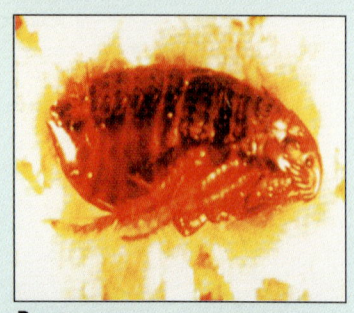

Pupa

Adult

Photos courtesy of Fleabusters Rx for fleas.

Flea Control

IGR (INSECT GROWTH REGULATOR)

Two types of products should be used when treating fleas—a product to treat the pet and a product to treat the home. Adult fleas represent less than 1% of the flea population. The pre-adult fleas (eggs, larvae and pupae) represent more than 99% of the flea population and are found in the environment; it is in the case of pre-adult fleas that products containing an Insect Growth Regulator (IGR) should be used in the home.

IGRs are a new class of compounds used to prevent the development of insects. They do not kill the insect outright, but instead use the insect's biology against it to stop it from completing its growth. Products that contain methoprene are the world's first and leading IGRs. Used to control fleas and other insects, this type of IGR will stop flea larvae from developing and protect the house for up to seven months.

EN GARDE: CATCHING FLEAS OFF GUARD!

Consider the following ways to arm yourself against fleas:

• Add a small amount of pennyroyal or eucalyptus oil to your dog's bath. These natural remedies repel fleas.
• Supplement your dog's food with fresh garlic (minced or grated) and a hearty amount of brewer's yeast, both of which ward off fleas.
• Use a flea comb on your dog daily. Submerge fleas in a cup of bleach to kill them quickly.
• Confine the dog to only a few rooms to limit the spread of fleas in the home.
• Vacuum daily...and get all of the crevices! Dispose of the bag every few days until the problem is under control.
• Wash your dog's bedding daily. Cover cushions where your dog sleeps with towels, and wash the towels often.

Health Care

product. This stimulates as many pupae as possible to hatch into adult fleas. The vacuum cleaner should also be treated with a flea treatment to prevent the eggs and larvae that have been hoovered into the vacuum bag from hatching.

The second stage of treatment is to apply an adult insecticide to the dog. Traditionally, this would be in the form of a collar or a spray, but more recent innovations include digestible insecticides that poison the fleas when they ingest the dog's blood. Alternatively, there are drops that, when placed on the back of the animal's neck, spread throughout the fur and skin to kill adult fleas.

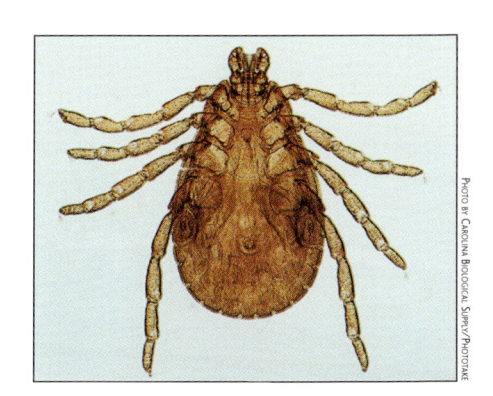

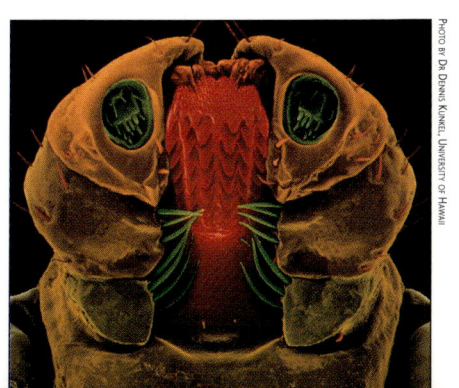

Dwight R Kuhn's magnificent action photo showing a flea jumping from a dog's back.

TICKS AND MITES

Though not as common as fleas, ticks and mites are found all over the tropical and temperate world. They don't bite, like fleas; they harpoon. They dig their sharp proboscis (nose) into the dog's skin and drink the blood. Their only food and drink is dog's blood. Dogs can get Lyme disease, Rocky Mountain spotted fever (normally found in the US only), paralysis and many other diseases from ticks and mites. They may live where fleas are found and they like to hide in cracks or seams in walls wherever dogs live. They are controlled the same way fleas are controlled.

A brown dog tick, *Rhipicephalus sanguineus*, is an uncommon but annoying tick found on dogs.

The head of a dog tick, *Dermacentor variabilis*, enlarged and coloured for effect.

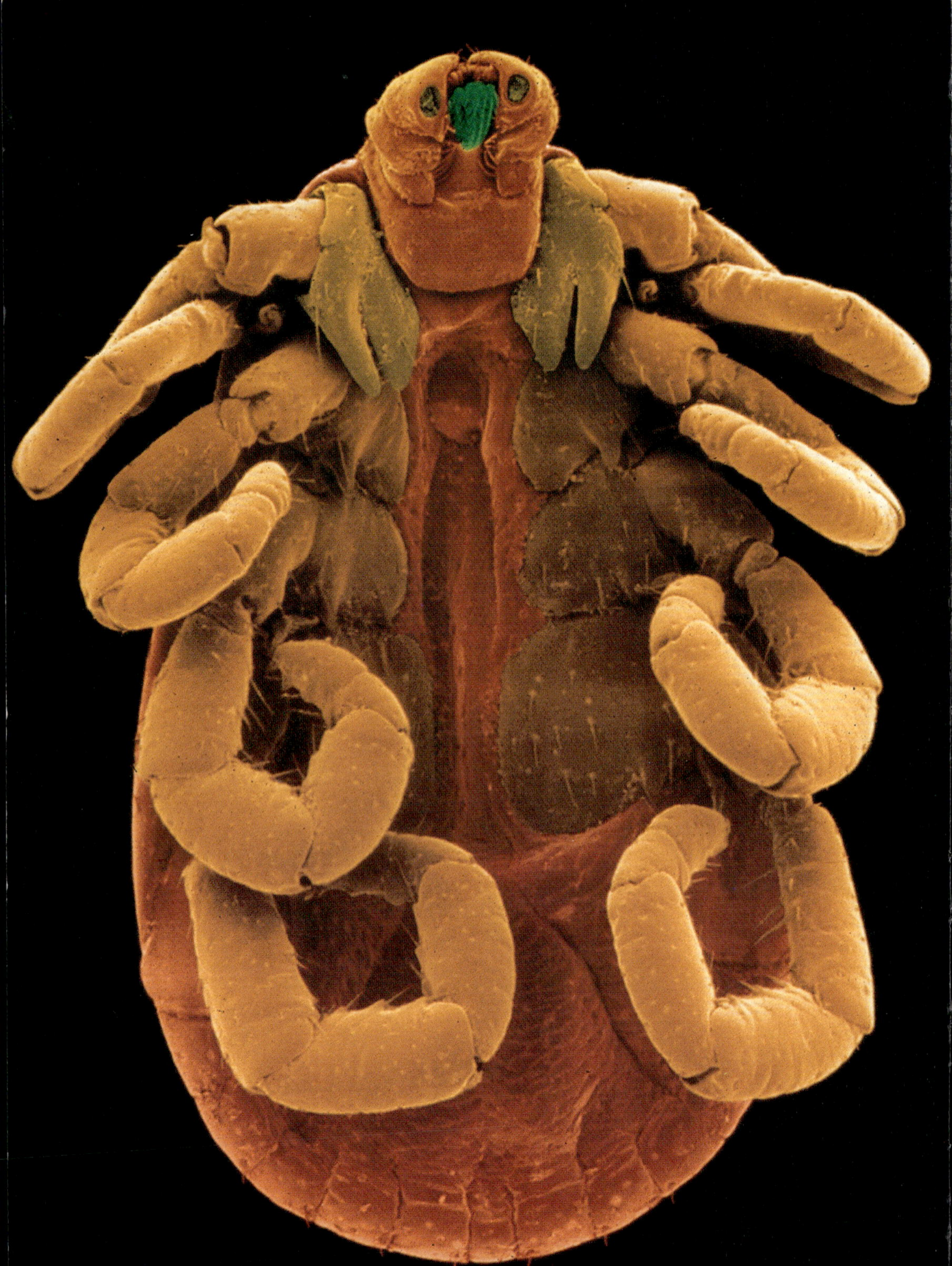

Health Care   139

The dog tick, *Dermacentor variabilis*, may well be the most common dog tick in many geographical areas, especially those areas where the climate is hot and humid.

Most dog ticks have life expectancies of a week to six months, depending upon climatic conditions. They can neither jump nor fly, but they can crawl slowly and can range up to 5 metres (16 feet) to reach a sleeping or unsuspecting dog.

BEWARE THE DEER TICK
The great outdoors may be fun for your dog, but it also is a home to dangerous ticks. Deer ticks carry a bacterium known as *Borrelia burgdorferi* and are most active in the autumn and spring. When infections are caught early, penicillin and tetracycline are effective antibiotics, but if left untreated the bacteria may cause neurological, kidney and cardiac problems as well as long-term trouble with walking and painful joints.

Opposite page: The dog tick, *Dermacentor variabilis*, is probably the most common tick found on dogs. Look at the strength in its eight legs! No wonder it's hard to detach them.

A deer tick, the carrier of Lyme disease. This magnified micrograph has been colorized for effect.

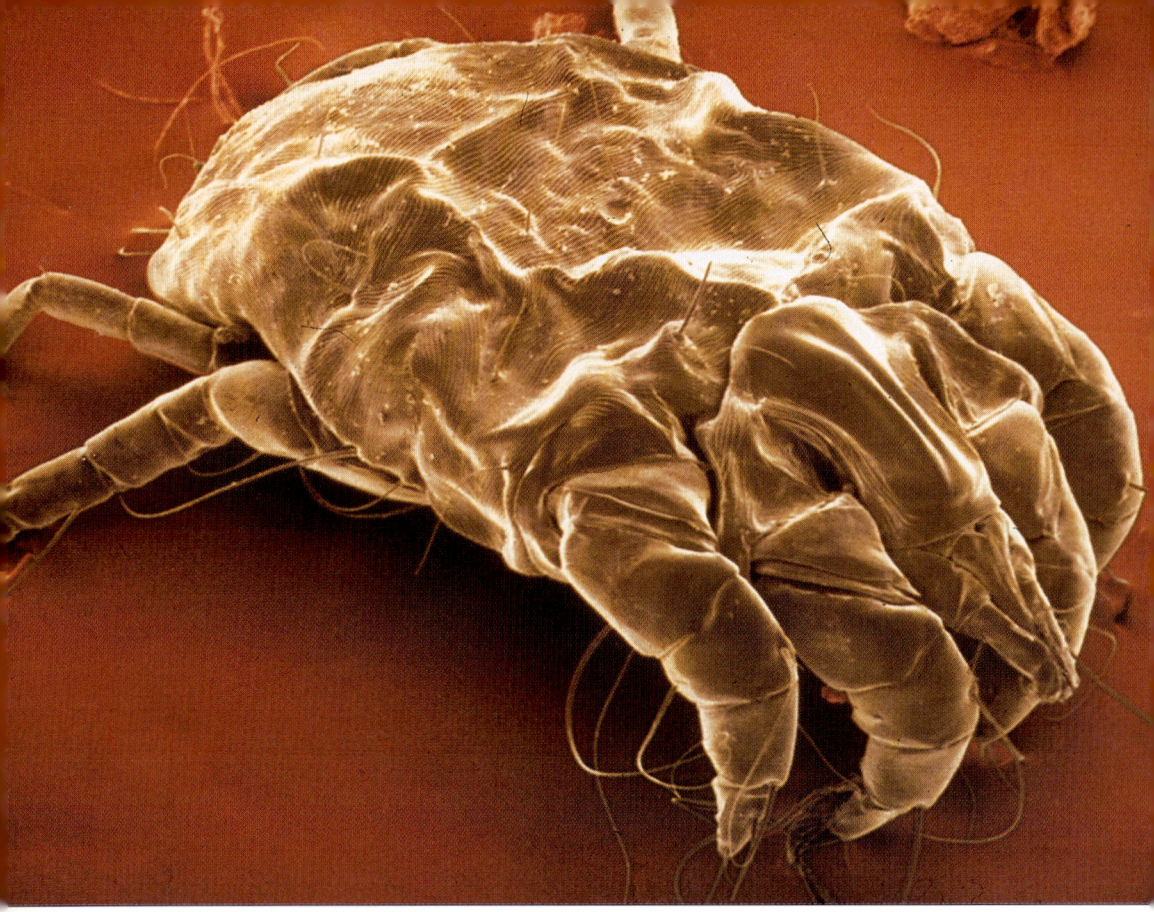

The mange mite, *Psoroptes bovis*.

Human lice look like dog lice; the two are closely related.

MANGE

Mites cause a skin irritation called mange. Some are contagious, like *Cheyletiella*, ear mites, scabies and chiggers. Mites that cause ear-mite infestations are usually controlled with Lindane, which can only be administered by a vet, followed by Tresaderm at home.

It is essential that your dog be treated for mange as quickly as possible because some forms of mange are transmissible to people.

Health Care

INTERNAL PARASITES

Most animals—fishes, birds and mammals, including dogs and humans—have worms and other parasites that live inside their bodies. According to Dr Herbert R Axelrod, the fish pathologist, there are two kinds of parasites: dumb and smart. The smart parasites live in peaceful cooperation with their hosts (symbiosis), while the dumb parasites kill their host. Most of the worm infections are relatively easy to control. If they are not controlled they weaken the host dog to the point that other medical problems occur, but they are not dumb parasites.

ROUNDWORMS

The roundworms that infect dogs are scientifically known as *Toxocara canis*. They live in the dog's intestines. The worms shed eggs continually. It has been estimated that a dog produces about 150 grammes of faeces every day. Each gramme of faeces averages 10,000–12,000 eggs of roundworms. There are no known areas in which dogs roam that do not contain roundworm eggs. The greatest danger of roundworms is that they infect people too! It is wise to have your dog tested regularly for roundworms.

Pigs also have roundworm infections that can be passed to humans and dogs. The typical roundworm parasite is called *Ascaris lumbricoides*.

The roundworm, *Rhabditis*. The roundworm can infect both dogs and humans.

ROUNDWORM

Average size dogs can pass 1,360,000 roundworm eggs every day.

For example, if there were only 1 million dogs in the world, the world would be saturated with 1,300 metric tonnes of dog faeces.

These faeces would contain 15,000,000,000 roundworm eggs.

It's known that 7–31% of home gardens and children's play boxes in the US contain roundworm eggs.

Flushing dog's faeces down the toilet is not a safe practice because the usual sewage treatments do not destroy roundworm eggs.

Infected puppies start shedding roundworm eggs at 3 weeks of age. They can be infected by their mother's milk.

DEWORMING

Ridding your puppy of worms is VERY IMPORTANT because certain worms that puppies carry, such as tapeworms and roundworms, can infect humans.

Breeders initiate a deworming programme at or about four weeks of age. The routine is repeated every two or three weeks until the puppy is three months old. The breeder from whom you obtained your puppy should provide you with the complete details of the deworming programme.

Your veterinary surgeon can prescribe and monitor the programme of deworming for you. The usual programme is treating the puppy every 15–20 days until the puppy is positively worm free.

It is advised that you only treat your puppy with drugs that are recommended professionally.

HOOKWORMS

The worm *Ancylostoma caninum* is commonly called the dog hookworm. It is dangerous to humans and cats. It also has teeth by which it attaches itself to the intestines of the dog. It changes the site of its attachment about six times a day and the dog loses blood from each detachment, possibly causing iron-deficiency anaemia. Hookworms are easily purged from the dog with many medications. Milbemycin oxime, which also serves as a heartworm preventative in Collies, can be used for this purpose.

In Britain the 'temperate climate' hookworm (*Uncinaria stenocephala*) is rarely found in pet or show dogs, but can occur in hunting packs, racing Greyhounds and sheepdogs because the worms can be prevalent wherever dogs are exercised regularly on grassland.

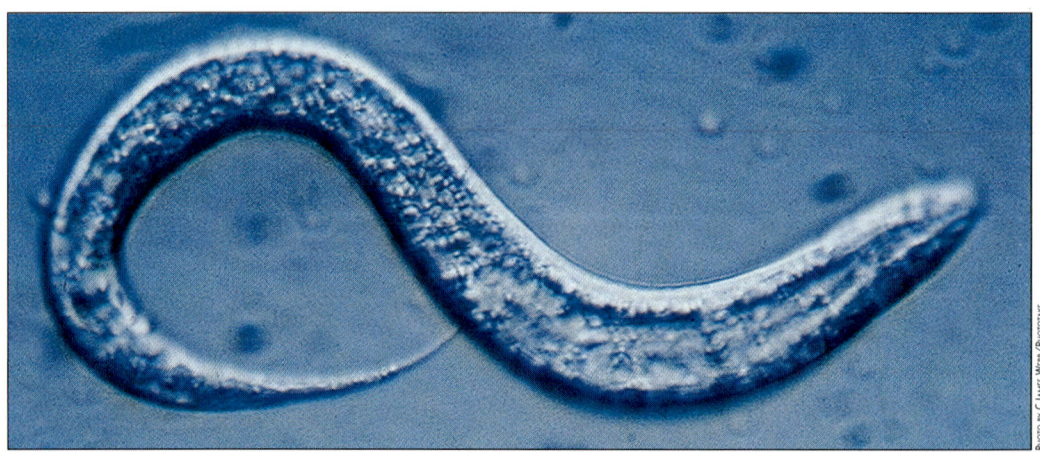

The infective stage of the hookworm larva.

Health Care **143**

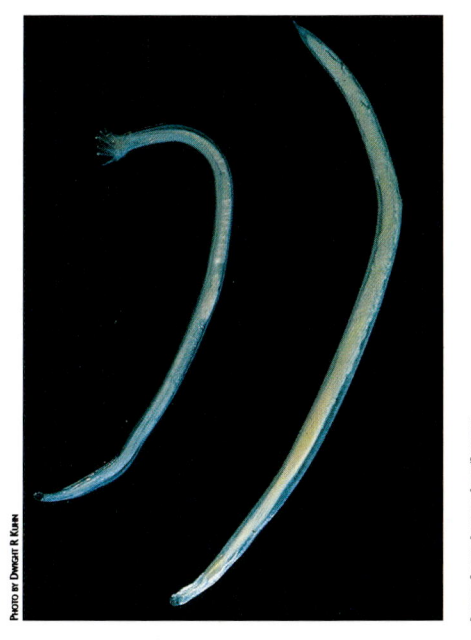

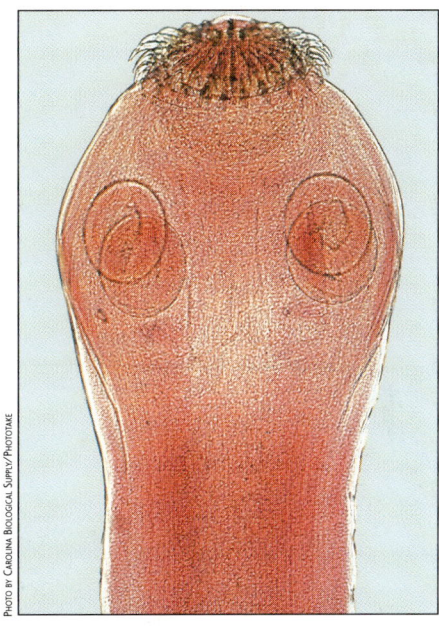

Left:
Male and female hookworms, *Ancylostoma caninum*, are uncommonly found in pet or show dogs in Britain. Hookworms may infect other dogs that have exposure to grasslands.

Right:
The head and rostellum (the round prominence on the scolex) of a tapeworm, which infects dogs and humans.

TAPEWORMS

There are many species of tapeworms. They are carried by fleas! The dog eats the flea and starts the tapeworm cycle. Humans can also be infected with tapeworms, so don't eat fleas! Fleas are so small that your dog could pass them onto your hands, your plate or your food and thus make it possible for you to ingest a flea which is carrying tapeworm eggs.

While tapeworm infection is not life threatening in dogs (smart parasite!), it can be the cause of a very serious liver disease for humans. About 50 percent of the humans infected with *Echinococcus multilocularis*, a type of tapeworm that causes alveolar hydatis, perish.

TAPEWORM

Humans, rats, squirrels, foxes, coyotes, wolves, mixed breeds of dogs and purebred dogs are all susceptible to tapeworm infection. Except in humans, tapeworms are usually not a fatal infection.

Infected individuals can harbour a thousand parasitic worms.

Tapeworms have two sexes—male and female (many other worms have only one sex—male and female in the same worm).

If dogs eat infected rats or mice, they get the tapeworm disease.

One month after attaching to a dog's intestine, the worm starts shedding eggs. These eggs are infective immediately.

Infective eggs can live for a few months without a host animal.

Heartworms

Heartworms are thin, extended worms up to 30 cms (12 ins) long which live in a dog's heart and the major blood vessels surrounding it. Dogs may have up to 200 worms. Symptoms may be loss of energy, loss of appetite, coughing, the development of a pot belly and anaemia.

Heartworms are transmitted by mosquitoes. The mosquito drinks the blood of an infected dog and takes in larvae with the blood. The larvae, called microfilaria, develop within the body of the mosquito and are passed on to the next dog bitten after the larvae mature. It takes two to three weeks for the larvae to develop to the infective stage within the body of the mosquito. Dogs should be treated at about six weeks of age, and maintained on a prophylactic dose given monthly.

Blood testing for heartworms is not necessarily indicative of how seriously your dog is infected. This is a dangerous disease. Although heartworm is a problem for dogs in America, Australia, Asia and Central Europe, dogs in the United Kingdom are not currently affected by heartworm.

The heart of a dog infected with canine heartworm, Dirofilaria immitis.

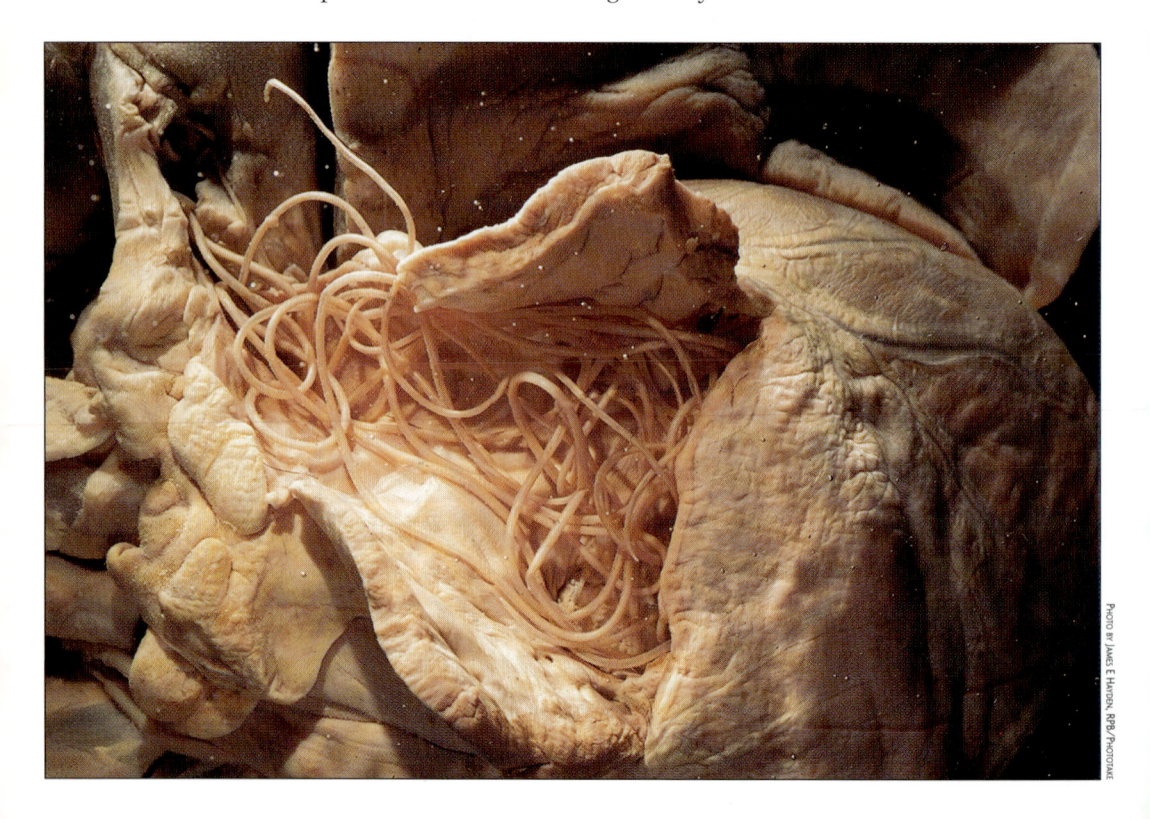

CDS
COGNITIVE DYSFUNCTION SYNDROME
'Old Dog Syndrome'

SYMPTOMS OF CDS

There are many ways to evaluate old-dog syndrome. Veterinary surgeons have defined CDS (cognitive dysfunction syndrome) as the gradual deterioration of cognitive abilities. These are indicated by changes in the dog's behaviour. When a dog changes its routine response, and maladies have been eliminated as the cause of these behavioural changes, then CDS is the usual diagnosis.

More than half the dogs over 8 years old suffer some form of CDS. The older the dog, the more chance it has of suffering from CDS. In humans, doctors often dismiss the CDS behavioural changes as part of 'winding down.'

There are four major signs of CDS: frequent toilet accidents inside the home, sleeps much more or much less than normal, acts confused, and fails to respond to social stimuli.

FREQUENT TOILET ACCIDENTS
- *Urinates in the house.*
- *Defecates in the house.*
- *Doesn't signal that he wants to go out.*

SLEEP PATTERNS
- *Moves much more slowly.*
- *Sleeps more than normal during the day.*
- *Sleeps less during the night.*

CONFUSION
- *Goes outside and just stands there.*
- *Appears confused with a faraway look in his eyes.*
- *Hides more often.*
- *Doesn't recognise friends.*
- *Doesn't come when called.*
- *Walks around listlessly and without a destination goal.*

FAILS TO RESPOND TO SOCIAL STIMULI
- *Comes to people less frequently, whether called or not.*
- *Doesn't tolerate petting for more than a short time.*
- *Doesn't come to the door when you return home from work.*

HOMEOPATHY:
an alternative to conventional medicine

'Less is Most'

Using this principle, the strength of a homeopathic remedy is measured by the number of serial dilutions that were undertaken to create it. The greater the number of serial dilutions, the greater the strength of the homeopathic remedy. The potency of a remedy that has been made by making a dilution of 1 part in 100 parts (or 1/100) is 1c or 1cH. If this remedy is subjected to a series of further dilutions, each one being 1/100, a more dilute and stronger remedy is produced. If the remedy is diluted in this way six times, it is called 6c or 6cH. A dilution of 6c is 1 part in 1000,000,000,000. In general, higher potencies in more frequent doses are better for acute symptoms and lower potencies in more infrequent doses are more useful for chronic, long-standing problems.

CURING OUR DOGS NATURALLY

Holistic medicine means treating the whole animal as a unique, perfect living being. Generally, holistic treatments do not suppress the symptoms that the body naturally produces, as do most medications prescribed by conventional doctors and vets. Holistic methods seek to cure disease by regaining balance and harmony in the patient's environment. Some of these methods include use of nutritional therapy, herbs, flower essences, aromatherapy, acupuncture, massage, chiropractic, and, of course the most popular holistic approach, homeopathy. Homeopathy is a theory or system of treating illness with small doses of substances which, if administered in larger quantities, would produce the symptoms that the patient already has. This approach is often described as 'like cures like.' Although modern veterinary medicine is geared toward the 'quick fix,' homeopathy relies on the belief that, given the time, the body is able to heal itself and return to its natural, healthy state.

Choosing a remedy to cure a problem in our dogs is the difficult part of homeopathy. Consult with your veterinary surgeon for a professional diagnosis of your dog's symptoms. Often these symptoms require immediate conventional care. If your vet is willing, and somewhat knowledgeable, you may attempt a homeopathic remedy. Be aware that cortisone prevents homeopathic remedies from working. There are hundreds of possibilities and combinations to cure many problems in dogs, from basic physical problems such as excessive moulting, fleas or other parasites, unattractive doggy odour, bad breath, upset tummy, dry, oily or dull coat, diarrhoea, ear problems or eye discharge (including tears and dry or mucousy matter), to behavioural abnormalities, such as fear of loud noises, habitual licking, poor appetite, excessive barking, obesity and various phobias. From alumina to zincum metallicum, the remedies span the planet and the imagination…from flowers and weeds to chemicals, insect droppings, diesel smoke and volcanic ash.

Using 'Like to Treat Like'

Unlike conventional medicines that suppress symptoms, homeopathic remedies treat illnesses with small doses of substances that, if administered in larger quantities, would produce the symptoms that the patient already has. Whilst the same homeopathic remedy can be used to treat different symptoms in different dogs, here are some interesting remedies and their uses.

Apis Mellifica
(made from honey bee venom) can be used for allergies or to reduce swelling that occurs in acutely infected kidneys.

Diesel Smoke
can be used to help control travel sickness.

Calcarea Fluorica
(made from calcium fluoride which helps harden bone structure) can be useful in treating hard lumps in tissues.

Natrum Muriaticum
(made from common salt, sodium chloride) is useful in treating thin, thirsty dogs.

Nitricum Acidum
(made from nitric acid) is used for symptoms you would expect to see from contact with acids such as lesions, especially where the skin joins the linings of body orifices or openings such as the lips and nostrils.

Symphytum
(made from the herb Knitbone, Symphytum officianale) is used to encourage bones to heal.

Urtica Urens
(made from the common stinging nettle) is used in treating painful, irritating rashes.

HOMEOPATHIC REMEDIES FOR YOUR DOG

Symptom/Ailment	Possible Remedy
ALLERGIES	Apis Mellifica 30c, Astacus Fluviatilis 6c, Pulsatilla 30c, Urtica Urens 6c
ALOPECIA	Alumina 30c, Lycopodium 30c, Sepia 30c, Thallium 6c
ANAL GLANDS (BLOCKED)	Hepar Sulphuris Calcareum 30c, Sanicula 6c, Silicea 6c
ARTHRITIS	Rhus Toxicodendron 6c, Bryonia Alba 6c
CATARACT	Calcarea Carbonica 6c, Conium Maculatum 6c, Phosphorus 30c, Silicea 30c
CONSTIPATION	Alumina 6c, Carbo Vegetabilis 30c, Graphites 6c, Nitricum Acidum 30c, Silicea 6c
COUGHING	Aconitum Napellus 6c, Belladonna 30c, Hyoscyamus Niger 30c, Phosphorus 30c
DIARRHOEA	Arsenicum Album 30c, Aconitum Napellus 6c, Chamomilla 30c, Mercurius Corrosivus 30c
DRY EYE	Zincum Metallicum 30c
EAR PROBLEMS	Aconitum Napellus 30c, Belladonna 30c, Hepar Sulphuris 30c, Tellurium 30c, Psorinum 200c
EYE PROBLEMS	Borax 6c, Aconitum Napellus 30c, Graphites 6c, Staphysagria 6c, Thuja Occidentalis 30c
GLAUCOMA	Aconitum Napellus 30c, Apis Mellifica 6c, Phosphorus 30c
HEAT STROKE	Belladonna 30c, Gelsemium Sempervirens 30c, Sulphur 30c
HICCOUGHS	Cinchona Deficinalis 6c
HIP DYSPLASIA	Colocynthis 6c, Rhus Toxicodendron 6c, Bryonia Alba 6c
INCONTINENCE	Argentum Nitricum 6c, Causticum 30c, Conium Maculatum 30c, Pulsatilla 30c, Sepia 30c
INSECT BITES	Apis Mellifica 30c, Cantharis 30c, Hypericum Perforatum 6c, Urtica Urens 30c
ITCHING	Alumina 30c, Arsenicum Album 30c, Carbo Vegetabilis 30c, Hypericum Perforatum 6c, Mezerium 6c, Sulphur 30c
KENNEL COUGH	Drosera 6c, Ipecacuanha 30c
MASTITIS	Apis Mellifica 30c, Belladonna 30c, Urtica Urens 1m
PATELLAR LUXATION	Gelsemium Sempervirens 6c, Rhus Toxicodendron 6c
PENIS PROBLEMS	Aconitum Napellus 30c, Hepar Sulphuris Calcareum 30c, Pulsatilla 30c, Thuja Occidentalis 6c
PUPPY TEETHING	Calcarea Carbonica 6c, Chamomilla 6c, Phytolacca 6c
TRAVEL SICKNESS	Cocculus 6c, Petroleum 6c

Recognising a Sick Dog

Unlike colicky babies and cranky children, our canine kids cannot tell us when they are feeling ill. Therefore, there are a number of signs that owners can identify to know that their dogs are not feeling well.

Take note for physical manifestations such as:

- unusual, bad odour, including bad breath
- excessive moulting
- wax in the ears, chronic ear irritation
- oily, flaky, dull haircoat
- mucous, tearing or similar discharge in the eyes
- fleas or mites
- mucous in stool, diarrhoea
- sensitivity to petting or handling
- licking at paws, scratching face, etc.

Keep an eye out for behavioural changes as well including:

- lethargy, idleness
- lack of patience or general irritability
- lack of appetite, digestive problems
- phobias (fear of people, loud noises, etc.)
- strange behaviour, suspicion, fear
- coprophagia
- more frequent barking
- whimpering, crying

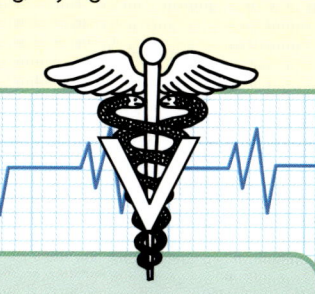

Get Well Soon

You don't need a DVR or a BVMA to provide good TLC to your sick or recovering dog, but you do need to pay attention to some details that normally wouldn't bother him. The following tips will aid Fido's recovery and get him back on his paws again:

- Keep his space free of irritating smells, like heavy perfumes and air fresheners.
- Rest is the best medicine! Avoid harsh lighting that will prevent your dog from sleeping. Shade him from bright sunlight during the day and dim the lights in the evening.
- Keep the noise level down. Animals are more sensitive to sound when they are sick.
- Be attentive to any necessary temperature adjustments. A dog with a fever needs a cool room and cold liquids. A bitch that is whelping or recovering from surgery will be more comfortable in a warm room, consuming warm liquids and food.
- You wouldn't send a sick child back to school early, so don't rush your dog back into a full routine until he seems absolutely ready.

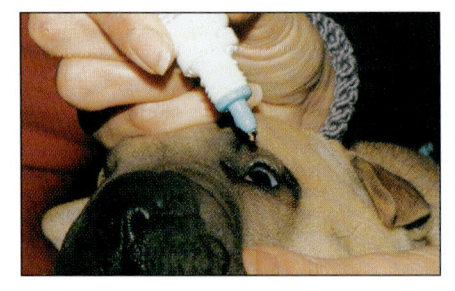

Your Shar Pei's eyes must be examined regularly and cared for by a veterinary surgeon. Clear, healthy eyes can only be produced by responsible breeders.

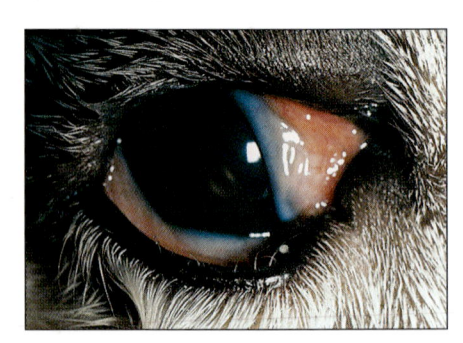

Lower entropion, or rolling in of the eyelid, is causing irritation in the left eye of this young dog. Several extra eyelashes, or distichiasis, are present on the upper lid.

A PET OWNER'S GUIDE TO COMMON OPHTHALMIC DISEASES
by Prof. Dr Robert L Peiffer, Jr.

Few would argue that vision is the most important of the cognitive senses, and maintenance of a normal visual system is important for an optimal quality of life. Likewise, pet owners tend to be acutely aware of their pet's eyes and vision, which is important because early detection of ocular disease will optimize therapeutic outcomes. The eye is a sensitive organ with minimal reparative capabilities, and with some diseases, such as glaucoma, uveitis and retinal detachment, delay in diagnosis and treatment can be critical in terms of whether vision can be preserved.

The causes of ocular disease are quite varied; the nature of dogs make them susceptible to traumatic conditions, the most common of which include proptosis of the globe, cat scratch injuries and penetrating wounds from foreign objects, including sticks and air rifle pellets. Infectious diseases caused by bacteria, viruses or fungi may be localized to the eye or part of a systemic infection. Many of the common conditions, including eyelid conformational problems, cataracts, glaucoma and retinal degenerations have a genetic basis.

Before acquiring your puppy it is important to ascertain that both parents have been examined and certified free of eye disease by a veterinary ophthalmologist. Since many of these genetic diseases can be detected early in life, acquire the pup with the condition that it pass a thorough ophthalmic examination by a qualified specialist.

LID CONFORMATIONAL ABNORMALITIES
Both entropion and ectropion are considerable problems in the Shar Pei. Entropion (rolling in) can involve the upper and/or lower lids. Signs usually appear between 3 and 12 months of age. The irritation caused by the eyelid hairs rubbing on the surface of the cornea may result in blinking, tearing and

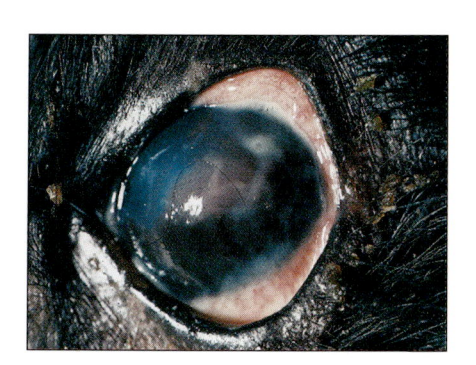

Health Care 151

Keratoconjunctivitis sicca, seen here in the right eye of a middle-aged dog, causes a characteristic thick mucous discharge as well as secondary corneal changes.

damage to the cornea. Ectropion (rolling out) is considered 'normal' in hounds but is abnormal in Shar Pei; unlike entropion, which results in acute discomfort, ectropion may cause chronic irritation related to exposure and the pooling of secretions. Most of these cases can be managed medically with daily irrigation with sterile saline and topical antibiotics when required. Eye tacking is common with Shar Pei puppies. Corrective surgery may be necessary in severe cases.

EYELASH ABNORMALITIES

Dogs normally have lashes only on the upper lids, in contrast to humans. Occasionally, extra eyelashes may be seen emerging at the eyelid margin (distichiasis) or through the inner surface of the eyelid (ectopic cilia).

CONJUNCTIVITIS

Inflammation of the conjunctiva, the pink tissue that lines the lids and the anterior portion of the sclera, is generally accompanied by redness, discharge and mild discomfort. The majority of cases are either associated with bacterial infections or dry eye syndrome. Fortunately, topical medications are generally effective in curing or controlling the problem.

DRY EYE SYNDROME

Dry eye syndrome (keratoconjunctivitis sicca) is a common cause of external ocular disease. Discharge is typically thick and sticky, and keratitis is a frequent component; any breed can be affected. While some cases can be associated with toxic effects of drugs, including the sulfa antibiotics, the cause in the majority of the cases cannot be determined and is assumed to be immune-mediated.

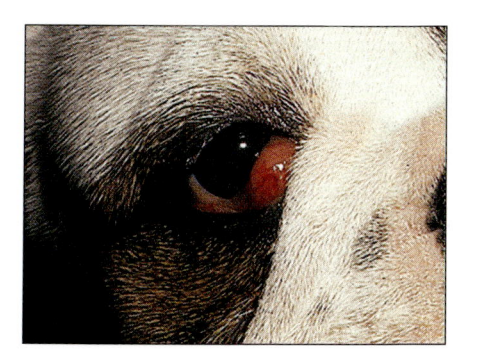

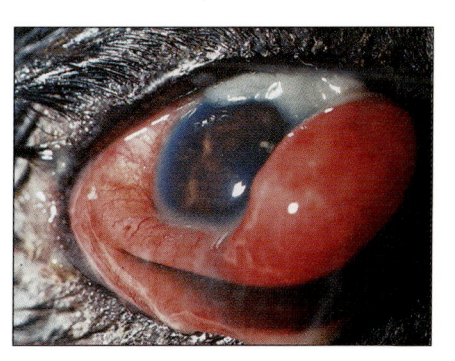

Left: Prolapse of the gland of the third eyelid in the right eye of a pup. Right: In this case, in the right eye of a young dog, the prolapsed gland can be seen emerging between the edge of the third eyelid and the corneal surface.

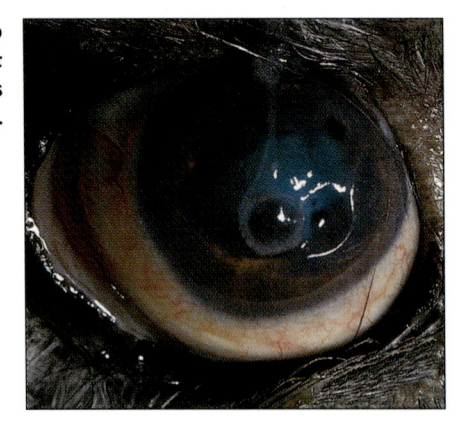

Multiple deep ulcerations affect the cornea of this middle-aged dog.

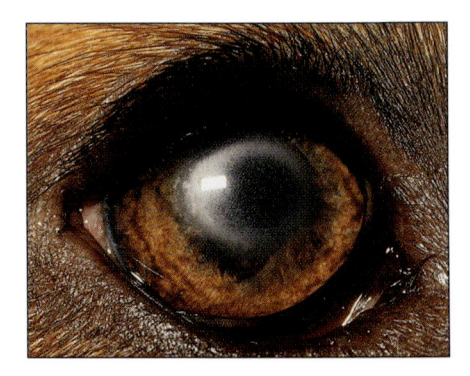

Lipid deposition can occur as a primary inherited dystrophy, or secondarily to hypercholesterolemia (in dogs frequently associated with hypothyroidism), chronic corneal inflammation or neoplasia. The deposits in this dog assume an oval pattern in the centre of the cornea.

Prolapse of the Gland of the Third Eyelid

In this condition, commonly referred to as *cherry eye*, the gland of the third eyelid, which produces about one-third of the aqueous phase of the tear film and is normally situated within the anterior orbit, prolapses to emerge as a pink fleshy mass protruding over the edge of the third eyelid, between the third eyelid and the cornea. The condition usually develops during the first year of life and, while mild irritation may result, the condition is unsightly as much as anything else.

Corneal Disease

The cornea is the clear front part of the eye that provides the first step in the collection of light on its journey to be eventually focused onto the retina, and most corneal diseases will be manifested by alterations in corneal transparency. The cornea is an exquisitely innervated tissue, and defects in corneal integrity are accompanied by pain, which is demonstrated by squinting.

Corneal ulcers may occur secondary to trauma or to irritation from entropion or ectopic cilia. In middle-aged or older dogs, epithelial ulcerations may occur spontaneously due to an inherent defect; these are referred to as indolent or Boxer ulcers, in recognition of the breed in which we see the condition most frequently. Infection may occur secondarily. Ulcers can be potentially blinding conditions; severity is dependent upon the size and depth of the ulcer and other complicating features.

Non-ulcerative keratitis tends to have an immune-mediated component and is managed by topical immunosuppressants, usually corticosteroids. Corneal edema can occur in elderly dogs. It is due to a failure of the corneal endothelial 'pump.'

The cornea responds to chronic irritation by transforming

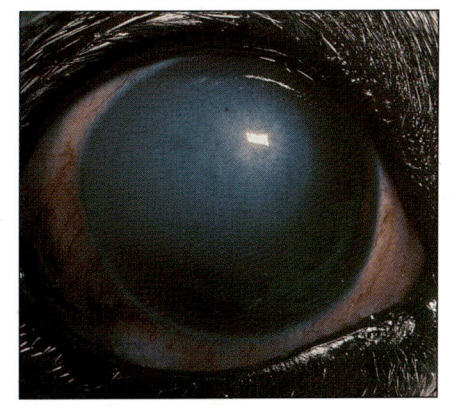

Health Care

into skin-like tissue that is evident clinically by pigmentation, scarring and vascularization; some cases may respond to tear stimulants, lubricants and topical corticosteroids, while others benefit from surgical narrowing of the eyelid opening in order to enhance corneal protection.

UVEITIS
Inflammation of the vascular tissue of the eye—the uvea—is a common and potentially serious disease in dogs. While it may occur secondarily to trauma or other intraocular diseases, such as cataracts, most commonly uveitis is associated with some type of systemic infectious or neoplastic process. Uncontrolled, uveitis can lead to blinding cataracts, glaucoma and/or retinal detachments, and aggressive symptomatic therapy with dilating agents (to prevent pupillary adhesions) and anti-inflammatories are critical.

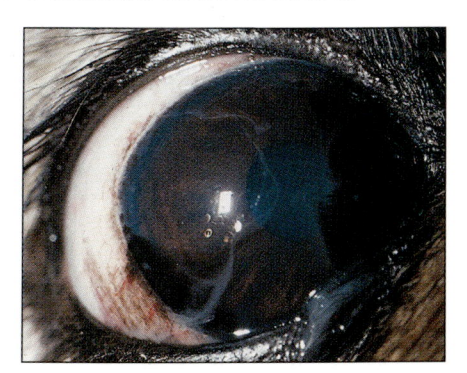

GLAUCOMA
The eye is essentially a hollow fluid-filled sphere, and the pressure within is maintained by regulation of the rate of fluid production and fluid egress at 10–20 mms of mercury. The retinal cells are extremely sensitive to elevations of intraocular pressure and, unless controlled, permanent blindness can occur within hours to days. In acute glaucoma, the conjunctiva becomes congested, the cornea cloudy, the pupil moderate and fixed; the eye is generally painful and avisual. Increased constant signs of

Corneal edema can develop as a slowly progressive process in elderly Boston Terriers, Miniature Dachshunds and Miniature Poodles, as well as others, as a result of the inability of the corneal endothelial 'pump' to maintain a state of dehydration.

Medial pigmentary keratitis in this dog is associated with irritation from prominent facial folds.

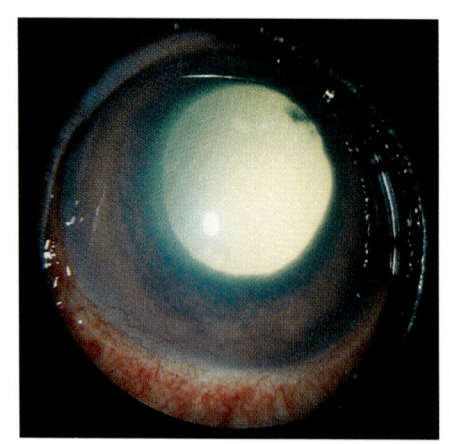

Glaucoma in the dog most commonly occurs as a sudden extreme elevation of intraocular pressure, frequently to three to four times the norm. The eye of this dog demonstrates the common signs of episcleral injection, or redness; mild diffuse corneal cloudiness, due to edema; and a mid-sized fixed pupil.

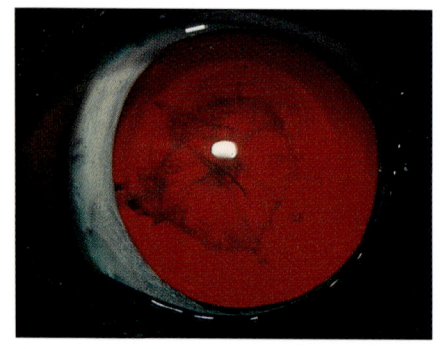

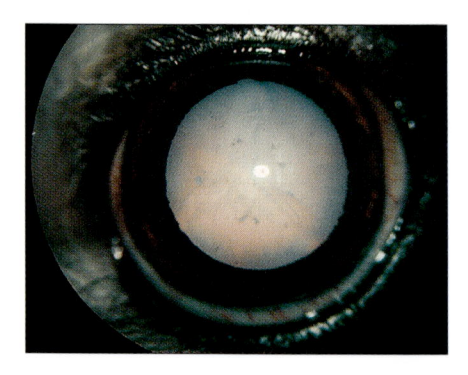

Left: The typical posterior subcapsular cataract appears between one and two years of age, but rarely progresses to where the animal has visual problems. Right: Inherited cataracts generally appear between three and six years of age, and progress to the stage seen where functional vision is significantly impaired.

discomfort will accompany chronic cases.

Management of glaucoma is one of the most challenging situations the veterinary ophthalmologist faces; in spite of intense efforts, many of these cases will result in blindness.

CATARACTS AND LENS DISLOCATION

Cataracts are the most common blinding condition in dogs; fortunately, they are readily amenable to surgical intervention, with excellent results in terms of restoration of vision and replacement of the cataractous lens with a synthetic one. Most cataracts in dogs are inherited; less commonly cataracts can be secondary to trauma, other ocular diseases, including uveitis, glaucoma, lens luxation and retinal degeneration, or secondary to an underlying systemic metabolic disease, including diabetes and Cushing's disease. Signs include a progressive loss of the bright dark appearance of the pupil, which is replaced by a blue-grey hazy appearance. In this respect, cataracts need to be distinguished from the normal ageing process of nuclear sclerosis, which occurs in middle-aged or older animals, and has minimal effect on vision.

Lens dislocation occurs in dogs and frequently leads to secondary glaucoma; early removal of the dislocated lens is generally curative.

RETINAL DISEASE

Retinal degenerations are usually inherited, but may be associated with vitamin E deficiency in dogs.

Health Care

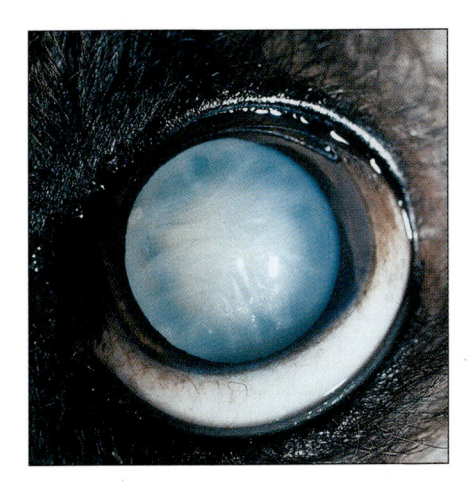

While signs are variable, most frequently one notes a decrease in vision over a period of months, which typically starts out as a night blindness. The cause of a more rapid loss of vision due to retinal degeneration occurs over days to weeks is labeled sudden acquired retinal degeneration or SARD; the outcome, however, is unfortunately usually similar to inherited and nutritional conditions, as the retinal tissues possess minimal regenerative capabilities. Most pets, however, with a bit of extra care and attention, show an amazing ability to adapt to an avisual world, and can be maintained as pets with a satisfactory quality of life. Detachment of the retina—due to accumulation of blood between the retina and the underling uvea, which is called the *choroid*—can occur secondarily to retinal tears or holes, tractional forces within the eye, or as a result of uveitis. These types of detachments may be amenable to surgical repair if diagnosed early.

OPTIC NERVE

Optic neuritis, or inflammation of the nerve that connects the eye with the brain stem, is a relatively uncommon condition that presents usually with rather sudden loss of vision and widely dilated non-responsive pupils.

Anterior lens luxation can occur as a primary disease in the terrier breeds, or secondarily to trauma. The fibres that hold the lens in place rupture and the lens may migrate through the pupil to be situated in front of the iris. Secondary glaucoma is a frequent and significant complication that can be avoided if the dislocated lens is removed surgically.

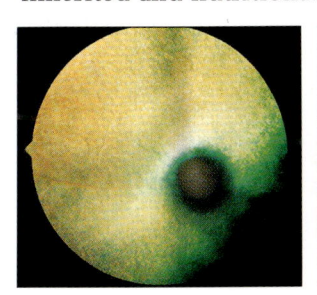

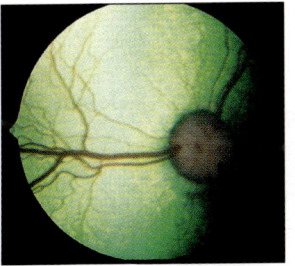

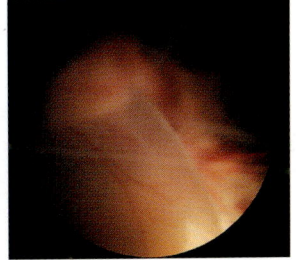

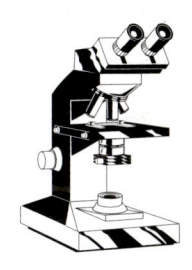

Left: The posterior pole of a normal fundus is shown; prominent are the head of the optic nerve and the retinal blood vessels. The retina is transparent, and the prominent green tapetum is seen superiorly.
Centre: An eye with inherited retinal dysplasia is depicted. The tapetal retina superior to the optic disc is disorganised, with multifocal areas of hyperplasia of the retinal pigment epithelium.
Right: Severe collie eye anomaly and a retinal detachment; this eye is unfortunately blind.

INDEX

*Page numbers in **boldface** indicate illustrations.*

Adult diet 72
Age 95
Aggression
—fear 114
Agility trials 114
AKC 17
Allergy 123
—airborne 128
—food 26129
—parasite bite 126
America 16
American Kennel Club 17
Amyloid protein 23
Ancylostoma caninum 142, **143**
Arthritis 28
Ascaris lumbricoides 141
Axelrod, Dr Herbert R 141
Backpacking 114
Bathing 78-79
Bear coats 21
Bedding 48
Bite 43
Bloat 69
Boarding 84
Bones 50
Bowls 53
Breed standard 30
—Hong Kong 35
Breeder 39-40, 42, 47
Britain 18
Brown dog tick **137**
Brush coats, 21
Canine parvovirus 126
Cat 103
Cataracts 154
Ch'ien Lung Dynasty 12
Ch'in Shih 9
Challenge Certificates 18
Chan, Joseph 36
Cherry eye **151**, 152
Chewing 98
Cheyletiella 140
Chinese Fighting Dog 16
Chinese Shar Pei 17

Chinese Shar-Pei Club of Great
    Britain 18
Chow Chow **10**, 12, 17
Chung, C M 16
Coat 21, 39
—care 76
—types 21
Collar 51, 103
—choke 53
Collie eye **155**
Colostrum 71
Colours 20
Come 108
Commands 97, 104
Communists 15
Conjunctivitis **151**
Corneal disease 152
Corneal edema **153**
Coronavirus 125
Crate 47, 49, 65, 83, 96, 99
—training 49, 99
Crufts Dog Show 18
Crying 65
Ctenocephalides **134**
Ctenocephalides canis **132-133**
Dah Let 10
Dah-Let Fighting Dog 11
Deer tick **139**
Demodectic mange 24
Dental health 81, 121
Dermacentor variabilis **137-138**,
    139
Dermatitis 26
Development schedule 95
Dew claws 10, 21
Deworming programme 142
Diet 70
—adult 72
—change in 73
—grain-based 71
—puppy 71
—senior 73
Dirofilaria immitis **144**
Discipline 101

Distemper 125
Distichiasis 151
Documents 41
Dog flea **132-134**, 135, **136-137**
Dog tick 137, **138**, 139
Dogs magazine 16
Down 105
Down-Homes Junoesque of
    Heathstyle 18
Dry eye syndrome 151
Ear care 81
Echinococcus multilocularis 143
Ectopic cilia 151
Ectropion 25, 151
Eczema 26
Entropion 24-25, **150**
Exercise 75, 84
External parasites 132-140
Eye
—care 81
—disease 150-155
—problems 24-25, 150
—tacking 25
—ulcers 25
Eyelash abnormalities 151
Familial Shar Pei fever 23
Fear aggression 114
Fear period 62
Fence 56
Fighting dogs 11
First aid 127, 145
Flea **132-134**, 135, **136-137**
—control 135-136
—life cycle 133, 136
Food 69
—allergy 26, 129
—intolerance 130
—preference 69
—proper diet 70
—storage 68
—treats 105, 112
Gastric torsion 69
Gender 64
Germany 19
Glaucoma 153, **154**
Grooming 76
—equipment 78
Han Dynasty 9, 14

Health
—dental 121
—problems 23
Heartworm **144**
Heathstyle Dandelion 18
Heel 110
Hepatitis 125
Hip dysplasia 28, **29**
Holistic medicine 146
Homeopathic remedies 26, 146 148
Hong Kong 16
—breed standard 35
—Kennel Club 21
Hookworm **142-143**
—larva **142**
Horse coats 21
Hot spots 128
Housebreaking 92
—schedule 99
Identification 86-87
Immune deficiency 27
Inherited retinal dysplasia **155**
Internal parasites 141-144
Kennel Club, The 18, 31, 41
—standard 33
Kennel cough 123, 125
Keratoconjunctivitis sicca **151**
Kuhn, Dwight R 137
Kwan Tung Province 10
Lead 50, 103
Lens dislocation 154
Lens luxation **155**
Leptospirosis 125
Lice 140
Ligget, Heather 18
Lindane 140
Litter 41
Long coats 21
Lucky 16
Lupus 128
Lyme disease 139
Mange 140
—demodectic 24
—mite 140
Mao Tse-tung 15
Matgo Law 16, 18
Midland Shar Pei Club 18
Milk 71
Ming Dynasty 15
Mite 137
Mucinosis 27
Nails 81
Neutering 124
Nipping 65
Nutrition 76
Obedience class 88, 113
Obedience school 114
Obesity 68, 76
Optic nerve 155
Optic neuritis 155
Overfeeding 68
Parasite
—bite 126
—external 132-140
—internal 141-144
Parvovirus 125
Personality 39
Pollen allergy 128
Preventative medicine 119
Prolapse of the gland **151**, 152
Psoroptes bovis **140**
Pug 14
Punishment 102
Puppy
—appearance 43
—family introduction 58
—financial responsibility 53
—first night home 59
—food 71
—health 123
—home preparation 46
—ownership 43
—problems 61-62, 64
—selection 38, 41-42
—training 63, 65, 90
Puppy-proofing 54, 56
Pyrenean Mountain Dog **10**, 11
Rabies 125
Rectal prolapse 27
Retinal disease 154
Retinal dysplasia **155**
Rhabditis **141**
Rhipicephalus sanguineus **137**
Roached back 24
Roundworm **141**, 142
SARD 155
Senior diet 73
Separation anxiety 65
Shar Pei fever 23
Shar Pei rash 27
Shar Pei syndrome 27
Sit 104
Skin problems 26-27, 125
—airborne 128
—auto-immune 126
—excessive licking 128
—hot spots 128
—parasite bites 126
Socialisation 40, 62-63
Soft palate elongation 26
Standard 21
Stay 107
Swollen hock syndrome 23
Systemic amyloidosis 23
Tai Leh 10
Tail 21
Tapeworm 142, **143**
Temperament 40
Thorndike's Theory of Learning 102
Thorndike, Dr Edward 102
Tibetan Mastiff 10, **12**
Tick 137, **138-139**
Toxocara canis 141
Toys 49, 51, 53
Tracheobronchitis 123
Training
—beginning 103
—consistency 104
—equipment 103
—puppy 63, 65, 90
Travelling
—air 84
—car 82
Treats 47, 103
Tresaderm 140
Tsang Pong Shing 14
Uncinaria stenocephala 142
Urinary tract disease 130
Uveitis 153
Vaccinations 66, 85, 121, 123
Veterinary surgeon 56, 117, 131, 135, 142
Water 74
Weinberg, Joachim 19
Whining 65
Wrinkle, The 18
Yuan 14

My Shar Pei

PUT YOUR PUPPY'S FIRST PICTURE HERE

Dog's Name _____

Date _____ Photographer _____